THE LITTLE BOOK OF GOOD HEALTH FACTS, TIPS & HABITS

Dr SONIA KAKAR

Orient Publishing
DELHI | MUMBAI | HYDERABAD

Disclaimer

The information included in this book is general in nature and for reference and guidance only. It is not a substitute for medical advice and the readers are urged to consult their doctor before taking decisions which are medical in nature. The publishers and/ or the author do not endorse any company or product mentioned in the book.

The logo and trademark 'Good Health First' are owned by Orient Paperbacks.

ISBN: 978-81-222-0522-0

The Little Book of Good Health: Facts, Tips & Habits

Subject: Health & Fitness / Reference

1st Published in 2012

Published by
Orient Publishing
(an imprint of Orient Paperbacks)
5A/8 Ansari Road, New Delhi-110 002
www.orientpublishing.com

Design by Vision Studio

Printed at
Saurabh Printers Pvt. Ltd., Noida, India

Cover Printed at
Ravindra Printing Press, Delhi-110 006, India

THE LITTLE BOOK OF

181 brilliant fact-based practical ideas from around the world.

GOOD HEALTH

True health is about total well-being, both inside and outside.

FACTS, TIPS & HABITS

Read the book at one short sitting and refer back to it, again and again.

~

'Your body is a temple, but only if you treat it as one.'

— *Astrid Alauda*

The Author

SONIA KAKAR is a well known health and nutrition consultant to several multinational corporations like Sanofi and Glaxo Smithkline Beecham, Eily Lily and Amway. She has also been associated with Sitaram Bhartia Institute of Science and Research, and several other leading hospitals of New Delhi. She writes actively for Rotary Delhi Central Club, *Prevention* and *Men's Health* magazines.

After her schooling from St. Thomas, New Delhi she enrolled for graduate and post graduate studies in Food and Nutrition and graduated at top of her class, both in BSc and MSc programmes, and then went on to earn her Doctorate from Lady Irwin College, Delhi University. For her academic brilliance she received both Smt. Bhanumati Memorial Prize and Dr. Y.K. Subrahmaniyam Memorial Prize.

She is a recipient of Senior Research Fellow Award of Indian Council of Medical Research and was recently appointed as the member of the Organizing Committee of the International Diabetes Federation WDC 2013. She has also been selected as National Faculty Member on Board with International Faculty for writing the curriculum to train 3000 allied health professionals in diabetes education.

She has contributed to several international and national journals and has been invited to as a speaker to international conferences. The focus of her ongoing work is nutritional, lifestyle and psycho-social management of diabetes.

She is happily married to Dr. Vaneet Kakar and lives in New Delhi.

Contents

Foreword

We live in a world increasingly dominated by technology; technology has intruded into every aspect of our daily life. Some would even say it has come to dictate our daily life. Without doubt technology has made our lives easier, more comfortable and opened up newer vistas for most of us. No one quite knows or would be bold enough to even hazard a guess about the next life-changing technological breakthrough.

In the technology-dominated fast-paced world, we consciously need to take a step back, pause, and contemplate about the lifestyle choices that we make (or do not make), and the possible long-term effect of our decisions; few would deny the need for a healthy lifestyle. This book by Sonia Kakar is an attempt to share global knowledge and information on what really is the correct and relevant definition of 'good health'. It is truism to repeat that 'health' is no longer limited to mere physical aspects. All of us have come to realise, accept and rediscover what our ancestors always knew — that health has many more dimensions to it than merely physical; the other equally important aspects being emotional, mental, social and spiritual. The information in the book — facts, tips and habits — is explained in simple, lucid language without any medical or scientific jargon. Each essay is complete in itself, and without any lengthy or diversionary explanations.

The book provides updated knowledge in an organized, readable and focused fashion on preventing serious disease, treating minor ailment and common-sense but significant steps you can take to maintain and rediscover good health. The author stresses that readers should adapt the principle 'Nip the evil in the bud' so that issues of health, in the broadest sense of the term, that maybe bothersome, such as sleepless nights, are either prevented or quickly remedied. Even the seemingly innocent and insignificant matter of selecting the correct footwear and the correct tooth-brush have been addressed.

Dr Kakar's experience in this area of health and healthy lifestyles and her ability to communicate her knowledge effectively makes this book an important resource for each one of us and an absolute-must for every household.

There is an Italian proverb which says, 'he who enjoys good health is rich, though he knows it not'. This book makes each one of us richer.

Dr. K.S. Bhandari

M.Sc.; Ph.D.; Dip.Sc.Edu. (U.K) A.T.Sc.E. (USSR)
Former UNESCO Consultant in Science Education
Founder Director of Education (SCERT), Delhi

The Solemn Pledge:
Hippocratic Oath

~

Hippocrates, often referred to as the 'Father of Medicine,' was an ancient Greek physician who is said to have lived according to outstanding moral values and ethical medical practice. Perhaps the greatest contribution made by Hippocrates to medicine is the Hippocratic Oath. For centuries, physicians recited this oath (either in original or in a modified version) at convocation ceremonies and upon entering medical practice.

Although the oath has been subject to much debate over the centuries, both in terms of its content and its author, it remains one of the most quoted documents in the history of medicine.

The significance of the Hippocratic Oath does not reside in its specific guidelines, but rather, in its symbolism of an ideal: the selfless dedication to the preservation of human life.

Here is the full oath:

> I swear by Apollo, the Healer, and by Aesculapius[1], by Hygeia[2] and Panacea[3], and by all gods and goddesses, making them my witnesses, that I will fulfill according to my power and judgment this oath and this covenant:
>
> I will look on him who taught me this art as I do my own parents, and will share with him my livelihood. If he be in need, I will give him money. I will hold his offspring as my own brethren, and will teach them this art, if they wish to learn it, without fee or written bond. I will give them instruction by precept and by

---

[1] Aesculapius — the Greek god of medicine and healing.

[2] Hygeia — the daughter of Aesculapius, she is the goddess and personification of health, cleanliness and sanitation.

[3] Panacea — another daughter of Aesculapius, goddess of universal remedy in Greek mythology.

lecture and by every other mode to my sons, to the sons of him who taught me, and to those pupils who have taken the covenant and sworn the physicians' oath, and to none other besides.

According to my power and judgment, I will prescribe regimen in order to benefit the sick, and do them no injury or wrong.

I will neither give or demand any deadly drug, nor prompt any such course, nor, similarly, will I give a destructive pessary to woman.

In holiness and righteousness I will pass my life and practice my art.

Into whatever houses I enter, my entrance shall be for the benefit of the sick, and shall be void of all intentional injustice or wrongdoing, especially of carnal knowledge of woman or man, bond or free.

And whatsoever, either in my practice or apart from it in daily life, I see or hear which should not be spoken of outside, thereon will I keep silence, judging such silence sacred.

If then I fulfill this oath and do not violate it, may I enjoy my life and art and be held in honor among all men for ever; but if I transgress and prove false to my oath, then may the contrary befall me.

Break One Unhealthy Habit

Pick just one habit you want to eliminate and take the first step to break it this very minute. Research shows that it takes about three weeks to replace an unhealthy habit with a healthy one.

The first step is to identify the habit you want to change. The second step is to identify one healthy habit that will replace the unhealthy habit you're giving up. Go for a brisk forty-five-minute walk three times a week, for example, instead of stopping for a few beers. Then identify the rewards you'll give yourself if you're successful in breaking the habit you've chosen.

Once you decide to break a habit, stick with your decision. The initial phase is the most difficult, but it will become easier and easier over time. So whenever you think that it's too difficult, just remember that it won't be so for long. You just have to keep moving forward.

Help yourself follow through with your plan by putting your commitment in writing.

The more changes you can make in your daily life to support quitting your bad habit and instilling good habits, the more successful you will be. Good luck!

See also: MAKE A PERSONAL HEALTH PLAN.

Be a Healthy Shopper

Nutrition experts and consumer advocates recommend that you follow these tips to be a healthy shopper.

Plan your healthy meals before you go shopping.

Write down what you need and take the list with you to the store.

Eat before you go to the market. If you're hungry, you may not be able to resist fat-laden goodies.

Avoid soft drinks, high-fat potato chips, candy, cake and ice cream.

Stick to fresh fruits and vegetables, whole grains, beans and other ingredients on your list.

Be careful! Every smart consumer knows that the stores place tempting items — which are not good for you — around the payment points to seduce you while you wait in line.

If you buy mainly processed foods, rethink your shopping habits. Processing generally destroys vitamins and other valuable nutrients. That's why fresh vegetables are generally better nutrition bargains than frozen or canned vegetables. And they usually cost less, too.

If you must buy processed foods, buy frozen rather than canned. Freezing destroys far fewer nutrients than canning.

So, next time you go shopping for foods choose only those that are good for the waistline and wallet.

See also: THE RAW FOOD DIET.

Save Your Skin from Stress

We turn red with embarrassment and white with fear. The skin, the largest organ of the human body, reflects all our emotions and can suffer because of them.

Being stressed out can be quite damaging for your skin. Stress actually causes a physiological reaction that results in the production of cortisol 'the stress hormone'. Cortisol causes inflammation. Inflamed pores on your skin clog more easily and can result in wrinkles. Hives, itching, eczema, rashes and psoriasis may be brought on or aggravated by stress.

When your skin breaks out, take a moment to sit quietly and ask yourself how you are really feeling. Are you angry? Do you feel there is too much pressure at work or at home? Do you feel guilty?

If you answer yes to any of these questions, and if your doctor determines that your skin problems are not caused by an infection, allergy or disease, regular practice of a relaxation technique may reduce stress and help keep your skin blemish-free. Ask your doctor for information about meditation, yoga, biofeedback and other methods that may help.

See also: QUICK FIXERS OR STRESS ENHANCERS; PRAY OR MEDITATE; PERSONALITY TYPES: A AND B; CRY BABY, CRY.

Make Love After a Heart Attack

Not only is it safe to have sex after a heart attack, but the pleasurable activity of making love is good for you, too! Just ask your doctor when you're recovered enough to give it a go — and whether or not you should take any medication to prevent chest pain during your activities.

Most people can safely return to sexual activity after recovering from a heart attack. Each person has a different timeline, depending on his or her level of physical discomfort, psychological readiness and previous level of sexual activity.

Many people worry that sex after a heart attack will be too strenous. However, there are several things you can do to make the experience less physically stressful. Foreplay not only is fun but also helps the heart gradually get ready for increased activity. And it's probably best to engage in sex when you are most relaxed — in the morning or perhaps after an afternoon nap.

The period of recovery from a heart attack can be a difficult time. But the pleasure, intimacy and emotional closeness that come from making love with your partner can help speed the healing process and bring peace of mind.

See also: TALK ABOUT SEX; EXERCISE YOUR 'MUSCLE OF LOVE'.

Adopt a Fertile Lifestyle

Infertility is a problem that is on the rise in many parts of the world and male infertility has been given more attention in recent years. If this is a concern of yours, consider making a few minor — but important — lifestyle changes before you rush off to see an expensive specialist.

The main problems in male infertility are sperm count, the mobility of the sperm produced and the quality of the sperm. Most cases of female infertility are caused by problems with ovulation. Without ovulation there are no eggs to be fertilized.

Alcohol, caffeine, cigarettes and 'recreational drugs' affect sperm count and ovulation. Using any of them can prevent you from becoming a parent.

A study conducted by the University of Surrey showed that couples with a previous history of infertility who made changes in their lifestyle, diet and took nutritional supplements had an 80 per cent success rate.

You may find it difficult to quit smoking, cut out coffee and stop drinking, but by doing so, you may find the easy answer to infertility.

See also: CUT DOWN ON CAFFEINE; FIGHT AGEING WITH ANTIOXIDANTS.

What Honey Can Do for You

Far from being just a tasty, sweet food, honey has some remarkable healing properties. In Hinduism, honey (*madhu*) is one of the five elixirs of immortality — *panchamrita*. In temples honey is poured over the deities in a ritual called *Madhu abhishekha*. The Islamic, Persian and other ancient traditions promote honey as a nutritious health food.

Containing approximately 150 biologically active ingredients, the healing properties of honey have been known to humanity for millennia. In the recent past the medical community has started to focus on this remarkable substance for its anti-bacterial and its anti-inflammatory properties — it is now being recommended to patients for the treatment of a wide range of health issues — from coughs and colds to stomach upsets and as a tonic. Interestingly many scientists have found a remarkable synergy between the result of their studies and the traditional usage of honey as a healing substance.

Honey is a powerful immune system booster due to its antioxidant and antibacterial properties. It contains as many antioxidants as spinach, apples, oranges or strawberries giving it a protective effect on the body. Raw honey contains several essential minerals like calcium, iron, sodium, phosphorous, sulphur and potassium, besides vitamins and protein.

The vitamins found in honey include vitamin C and B. The amount of vitamins change according to the qualities of the nectar and pollen the honey is made from.

Unprocessed or raw honey has the greatest healing properties, as pollen which contains the most active components of the honey is destroyed during processing and exposure to light. While all types of honey have some medicinal

properties, in general, darker shades have more antioxidants. These precious properties help to eliminate free radicals in the body that have been linked to several diseases, including cancer.

Famously, because of its anti-microbial properties, honey is used to relieve sore throats, either in a hot drink or by the spoonful.

One spoon of fresh honey, mixed with the juice of half a lemon in a glass of lukewarm water and taken first thing in the morning, is an effective remedy for constipation and hyperacidity. Fasting on this honey-lemon juice water is highly beneficial in the treatment of obesity without loss of energy and appetite.

Honey is an effective antidote to combat hangover from too much alcohol. It is gentle on the stomach and contains a mix of natural sugar — fructose — which speed up the oxidation of alcohol by the liver and act as a 'sobering' agent.

The benefits of honey might seem old fashioned, but they are proven, time-tested and increasingly backed by medical research.

Break the Rules, Once in a While

Obsessing over food rules is bad for your happiness, and probably your health, too. Over the past few decades, dieting and worrying too much about nutrition has made us no healthier or slimmer; cultivating a relaxed attitude towards food is important. It is important to enjoy your food since this stimulates the secretion of saliva which is essential for good digestion.

There will be special occasions when you will want to throw healthy eating rules out the window. What matters more are the habits that govern your eating on a typical day. 'All things in moderation' is often said, but we should never forget the wise addendum, sometimes attributed to Oscar Wilde: 'Including moderation.'

Worry for Thirty Minutes

Millions of people worry away long stretches of the day. And most worries are about things that never happen. Yet while people worry about what might happen — developing health problems related to anxiety along the way — life slips by unlived.

A Pennsylvania State University psychologist has developed a practical plan that can help you reduce the time you spend worrying. Among his suggestions are two that can free up a great deal of time for enjoying life. First, set aside thirty minutes a day for worrying. And second, write down a list of things to worry about during that period.

Another useful way to outwit worry is to use symbolism to get rid of it. The late Lord Rank, an outstanding British industrialist, rather whimsically used a little game he played to reduce the impact of worry. He organised what he called the 'Wednesday Worry Club.' He was the sole member. Instead of worrying every day, whenever a worry cropped up he would write it on a piece of paper and drop it in a box to be worried about on Wednesday afternoon at four o'clock, the meeting time of the 'club.'

At that time, he would empty all the deposited worries on a table. In going over them, always about 90 per cent had solved themselves and no longer needed to be worried about. 'But, what do you do with the other 10 per cent?' asked his friend Norman Vincent Peale.

'I put them back in the box to be worried about next Wednesday at four o'clock,' blandly replied Lord Rank.

These suggestions can be your first step to limiting — and then eliminating — needless worry in your life.

Therapeutic Oil of the Gods

Olive oil is the king of oils. It has been more than a mere food to the people of Mediterranean; it has been medicinal, magical, an endless source of fascination and wonder and the foundation of great wealth and power. Homer, the greatest ancient Greek epic poet called it 'Liquid Gold'.

Research has now confirmed what Mediterranean people always knew — that olive oil is highly beneficial for health and helps you to stay young.

Olive oil is a natural juice which preserves the taste, aroma, vitamins and properties of the olive fruit. It is the only vegetable oil that can be consumed as it is — freshly pressed from the fruit. Olive oil being almost pure fat, is dense in calories yet healthy and without adverse health effects.

Olive oil is high in monounsaturated fatty acids (MUFA). 'MUFAs help cut bad cholesterol and increase good cholesterol in our bodies, thereby reducing the risk of coronary diseases,' says Priya Jain, dietitian at Mumbai's Hinduja Hospital. 'It also improves insulin sensitivity, lowers blood sugar levels and lowers insulin requirement in diabetics.'

Olive oil helps to keep the arteries supple and contains the major fatty acid present in the oil of skin glands. This accounts for Mediterranean people having smooth, slightly oily skin, shiny hair which remain dark for most of their lives.

Olive oil is very well tolerated by the stomach. In fact, olive oil's protective function has a beneficial effect on ulcers and gastritis.

One US study suggests that oleic acid, the main MUFA in olive oil, reduces the expression of the gene associated with breast cancer. Phenols present in olive oil also protect against cancers of the colon, stomach and skin.

Olive oil is an excellent source of Vitamin E, a powerful antioxidant. 'Vitamin E in olive oil fights age-related problems by keeping a check on any deterioration of muscular control and mental faculties,' says Jain. 'And it's a concentrated source of other antioxidants.'

The process of extraction from olives results in different grades of oils. These include:

Extra Virgin Olive Oil is derived from the first pressing of olives without chemical treatments, it is superior in taste and aroma and has an acid content below 1 per cent. Considered the finest, it is also the most expensive and mostly used on breads or in salads.

Virgin Olive Oil is extracted from the second pressing of olives, it is also free from chemicals. It has an acid content of only 2 per cent.

Pure Olive Oil is obtained by refining and the methods used for it (heat, chemical solvents, high pressure and filtration) do not lead to alterations in the initial structure. It is later mixed with virgin olive oil to enhance aroma and flavour. This, unlike the virgin oils, is better for frying or cooking.

Olive Pomace Oil uses the pomace, the pulpy residue got after extraction, which is treated further with solvents and other physical methods. Virgin olive oil is then added. Much of the nutrients are lost during refining and so it is considered the least healthful variety. It's also the cheapest.

Olive oil is best stored tightly sealed, in a cool and dark place. Light and heat are the number one enemy of oil. Oxygen promotes rancidity. Like other oils olive oil can easily go rancid when exposed to air, light or high temperatures.

Even olive oil is high in calories, so it is best used in moderation. Remember, that you cannot make unhealthy foods healthier simply by adding olive oil in them.

See also: FATS: THE GOOD AND THE BAD; SLASH THE FAT; ADOPT AN ESKIMO DIET.

Keeping Your Brain Young

You probably don't give it much thought, but your brain needs good nutrition, workout, and good sleep, as much as any other major muscle group — only these can help boost creativity, memory and keep the brain young.

Excess dietary fat, especially saturated fat, usually clogs the arteries reducing the blood flow to the brain and causing it to age prematurely. Conversely, the lower the saturated fat in your diet, the body will eventually flush out the excess fat from your arteries restoring normal blood supply to the brain, for its rejuvenation.

A healthy diet rich in colourful fruit, omega-3 fatty acids and whole grains aids improved functioning of the brain. Fruits and vegetables are rich in vitamins, minerals and antioxidants which benefit brain chemistry. Coloured vegetables and fruits, walnuts, flax seeds, green tea, fish etc. are brain food in the real sense.

Exercise seems to support brain the same way as it helps cardiac health; by improving the blood flow which means more oxygen and nutrients reach the brain cells and sustain their optimal functioning.

A good night's sleep is immensely de-stressing and good for your brain. Stress hormones which get released in response to mental stress can have a negative impact on the brain. Putting away all your gadgets — phone, remote, tablet etc. — and enjoying a little time relaxing during the day is a good idea.

Mental games are fun, challenging and competitive — a great way to exercise your mind. Activities that make you think support new brain cell growth. Do the crossword or play the sudoku to keep your mind nimble. When it comes to brain fitness, the bottom line is 'to use it or lose it'.

Cry Baby, Cry

Most of us have a good cry from time to time, though some of us are like a rock and never or hardly ever cry. We should cry occasionally because crying is actually healthy in numerous ways.

Research into crying has revealed its many benefits. It helps relieve the physical tension that builds up when you're under stress. And researchers at Cornell University also argue that crying affects the central nervous system, restoring it to a state of balance by easing the stress you feel.

Crying is associated with an emotional response, when tears are shed, the endocrine system releases endorphins ('feel-good' hormones) that stabilize the mood. When we cry, we give our bodies the ability to stabilize and become content again.

In other words, crying seems to be an emotional safety valve that opens when the inner pressure is too great to handle.

Tears help to lubricate the eyes, keeping them functioning better by not allowing them to dry out.

It also seems that all forms of crying are not of equal value in terms of emotional relief. It appears that the chemistry of tears produced when cutting onions is different from that of tears produced by true sorrow.

So next time you feel like crying, yield to nature. Afterward, you'll be glad you did.

See also: CHOOSE TO BE HAPPY; LAUGH — LIFE IS SHORT.

Don't Give Aspirin to a Child with a Fever

Never give aspirin to a child who appears to have symptoms of a cold, the flu or chicken pox. Use acetaminophen (also called paracetamol) or nothing at all.

A deadly health problem, Reye's syndrome, is associated with aspirin use in children with the flu or chicken pox. Because it is difficult for a parent or an adult caregiver to know the cause of a

child's aches, pains and fever, it is important not to take any risks.

Reye's syndrome can produce serious damage to the brain and liver. At first, the flu or chicken pox may seem to be going away. But then persistent vomiting, confusion, extreme fatigue, seizures and personality changes set in. If the condition goes untreated, coma and even death can occur.

The safest course of action is to not give children aspirin if they have a fever. This will prevent Reye's syndrome from occurring.

The Drug Controller General, Government of India, recommends that aspirin should never be given to children under 12 years of age.

See also: NEVER MIX ASPIRIN AND VITAMIN C; HOW DOES ASPIRIN BENEFIT THE HEART; TREAT YOUR CHILDREN WELL.

Adopt an Eskimo Diet

A study looking for a link between Eskimos and their low incidence of heart disease focussed attention on the Eskimo diet, which is rich in fish.

The study indicated that the cold-water fish Eskimos eat protects them against cardiovascular disease. Cold-water fish are loaded with omega-3 fatty acids, substances that appear to reduce cholesterol and triglycerides in the blood, reduce the swelling from rheumatoid arthritis and prevent the blood clots that can trigger a heart attack or stroke.

You can get these potent nutrients from supplements or fatty fish. Plan two or three fish servings each week. According to Mayo Clinic researchers this could reduce your risk of heart disease by one third. Examples of fish high in beneficial omega-3s include anchovies, bass, herring, salmon, rohu, sardines, trout (rainbow and lake) *singhara* and tuna (especially white, albacore and bluefin).

Omega-3s are also present in some plants. Good plant sources include canola oil; ground flaxseed and flaxseed oil; whole soybeans and soybeans oil; tofu and walnuts (whole and oil).

Another option for vegetarians is to consider taking fish oil capsules. However, these capsules do not compensate fully for the benefits of actually eating fish.

In the words of Dr. William B Kannel of Boston University Medical School and the founder of Framingham Heart Study, 'My advice is to eat whole fish rather than fish oil, since you get a meal out of it.'

See also: KNOW YOUR CHOLESTEROL; SLASH THE FAT; THERAPEUTIC OIL OF GODS.

Fight Ageing with Antioxidants

Antioxidants are vitamins, minerals and enzymes that protect the body by neutralizing free radicals — the chemical molecules that can harm your health and accelerate ageing. Research has shown that certain foods contain antioxidants, which help the body defend itself against free radicals. Antioxidants also help your body ward off diseases, strengthen the immune system and help you keep looking younger.

Antioxidants — beta-carotene, vitamins C and E, plus the mineral selenium — can easily be increased in your diet by increasing the consumption of fruits, nuts and vegetables.

Asparagus, cantaloupe, carrots, dried apricots, green beans, peaches, spinach, sweet potatoes and tomato juice are abundant in beta-carotene.

Vitamin C is found in broccoli, brussels sprouts, cantaloupe, grapefruit juice, green peppers, orange juice, oranges and papaya; almonds, hazelnuts, wheat germ and oil, sunflower seeds and oil are full of vitamin E.

Selenium is found in broccoli, cabbage, onions, seafood and whole-grain cereals and breads.

Keep in mind that the fresher the food and lower the heat to which it is exposed, the higher its nutrient content.

While the use of antioxidants to slow down or prevent the ageing process makes sense, studies have yet to conclusively validate it. Taking large doses of some antioxidants, such as vitamin E may actually be harmful. A doctor's supervision is important to determine proper supplementary dose of antioxidants, if at all, to lower the risk of side effects.

See also: EAT YOUR COLOURS; THE RAW FOOD DIET.

Go Where You've Never Gone Before

The next time you're alone, sit back and relax. Then think: Is there something you've always wanted to do but put off for one reason or another?

Almost everyone has a dream that has been denied, whether it's to go back to college, go to Paris, return to the birthplace of parents, learn to play the sitar, study acting or take up painting. And now may be just the time to do it or to lay the groundwork for making that dream come true.

No matter who you are or where you live, there's some place you have promised yourself you'd go... someday! Make that someday today. Be spontaneous. Being spontaneous adds to the pleasure of being alive. And it stimulates your body to produce chemicals that keep you healthy and vigorous. Go yourself or pack your spouse and kids in the car and head out.

A deep dream finally lived out can renew the life force in you and do more for your health, appearance and self-esteem than any drug, technique or cosmetic ever can.

Millions of Indians have never been to the Taj Mahal or back waters of Kerala, or Leh or Jagannath Puri or Kashmir. Or even visited a nearby lake, a park, a museum or just the old neighbourhood where they grew up. Whatever the place, go there and enjoy the experience — and the journey.

You may need to save money or get more information, or you may be able to take action right now. Whatever the situation, make your dream come true — and enjoy the benefits that come with it.

See also: CHOOSE TO BE HAPPY.

Flatulence: Treatment & Prevention

A standard dictionary explanation of flatulence is 'presence of excessive gas in the digestive tract'. When this gas is expelled in the wind form it is called flatulence.

Flatulence might be embarrassing, but it is totally natural and normal, although it can result in an uncomfortable feeling of bloating.

Preventing flatulence is easy. It is usually a result of incomplete digestion. What you might want to do is to simply avoid or eat less of foods that lead to such a condition.

Foods such as dairy products, certain vegetables like beans, cabbage, cauliflower, broccoli, corn and fruits like apples, pears, peaches and prunes can cause some people to have excessive gas.

Foods that produce minimal gas include rice, bananas, citrus fruits, grapes, eggs, yogurt and non-carbonated drinks.

Excessive gas is often produced after eating high fat meal. The solution is to eat smaller, more frequent meals rather than 2 or 3 large meals, and avoiding high fat meals. Don't overeat. Keep the stomach one-third empty after a meal.

Some people tend to swallow air while they eat. They are usually unaware of this and the cause maybe hurried eating or anxiety. Being aware that air is being swallowed helps; the solution is to eat slowly and chew the food thoroughly.

Cooking also helps in reducing some of the offending

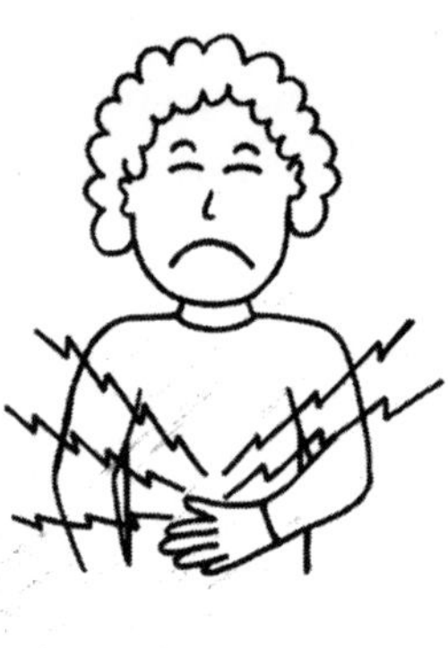

gas-producing ingredients in the food. The gas-producing potential in beans can be decreased by boiling them briefly and then letting them soak or just by cooking them longer. Steaming the beans and other 'gassy' food is always a good idea.

Drinking water or liquids half-an-hour before the meals instead of drinking with the meals, helps in better break-down and digestion of the food.

Since flatulence is also a result of poor digestion, developing habits and routines that help the stomach to digest better is a good idea. A short walk after eating is a definite help for better digestion. Lying down after eating is a definite no-no.

Keep in mind that almost any food or combination of foods don't get along together in certain people. Some people may say they feel bloated if they eat fruits with proteins, or when they eat proteins and starches together. It is person-specific and requires keeping track to trace the offending food. Once you discover such foods, eliminate them from your diet or eat them in small portions. The ultimate key is to follow the old advice — everything in moderation.

See also: FEAST ON FIBRE; THE DOCTOR IN YOUR KITCHEN; DON'T APOLOGIZE FOR EATING BEANS; PAY ATTENTION TO YOUR BODY'S SIGNALS; WHEN STOMACH DISAGREES.

Choose Sunglasses with UV Coating

Look for the 'UV100' tag on any pair of sunglasses you buy. It's your guarantee that your eyes are protected from the premature ageing caused by ultraviolet rays.

Fewer than half of the sunglasses on the market have adequate protection from ultraviolet light, so you have to be careful.

Many people think that dark glasses provide protection — and the darker, the better. But dark lenses without UV coating may be more dangerous to your eyes than wearing no sunglasses at all. Dark glasses cause your pupils to dilate. And with your pupils opened more widely, you're likely to receive an even larger dose of ultraviolet radiation than if you weren't wearing sunglasses at all.

Colour counts for more than looks in sunglasses. You may want to choose blue shades because they are in fashion or look more stylish, but they can be dangerous.

According to an eye specialist at the Manhattan Eye, Ear and Throat Hospital in New York City, you are better off with lenses that are tinted yellow or amber. These lenses are more protection of your eyes because they transmit yellow light, which is less damaging than the blue light transmitted by blue lenses.

Grey is a popular neutral tint that allows eyes to perceive colours in their purest form and reduce brightness and glare. Brown tinted glasses heighten contrast and visual acuity, while blocking blue light.

Good lenses don't need to be expensive. You can pick up one in consultation with the doctor. Take sunglasses that will provide effective protection against damaging rays.

See also: DRY EYES AND WATERY EYES; CONTACT LENSES VS GLASSES.

Choose to Be Happy

We convince ourselves that life will be better after we get married, have a baby, then another. Then we are frustrated that the kids aren't old enough and we'll be more content when they are. After that, we're frustrated that we have teenagers to deal with. We will certainly be happy when they are out of that stage. We tell ourselves that our life will be complete when our spouse gets his or her act together, when we get a nice car, are able to go on a nice vacation, when we retire.

The truth is, there's no better time to be happy than right now. If not now, when?

There's a saying you can use to help you change what you believe: 'You can't change the wind, but you can adjust your sails.' In other words, you can learn to respond to life's travails in a way that meets your needs. You can't change what happens, but you can change how you react to events.

Cognitive therapists have shown that most of us have 'learned helplessness' — that is, we come to expect disappointment, rejection and so on. But these researchers have also proved that we can learn optimism. We can learn to change our thinking patterns. It may not be as important to know how you reached your current state of mental health as it is to understand that you can take control of your own attitudes and life perspectives — now!

See also: CHERISH YOUR FRIENDS; GO WHERE YOU'VE NEVER GONE BEFORE; PAT, PURR AND PLAY WITH YOUR PET; LAUGH — LIFE IS SHORT; GET OUT OF THE RUT.

Bad Breath: Here's How to Make it Fresh

Because fresh breath is important to us, makers of mints and mouthwashes sell millions of dollars worth of products every year. However, these products are only temporarily helpful; they actually may be less effective than simply rinsing your mouth with water and brushing and flossing teeth regularly.

There are many causes of bad breath. *First,* your mouth itself may be the source. Bacterial breakdown of food particles and other debris in and around your teeth can cause a foul odour.

Second, a dry mouth, such as that occurs during sleep or as a result of some drugs or smoking, enables dead cells to accumulate on the tongue, gums and cheeks. As a result, they decompose and cause odour.

Third, eating foods with a strong odour causes bad breath. Onions, garlic are the best examples, but other vegetables, spices and oils may also cause bad breath.

Fourth, chronic infections in the lungs can produce foul-smelling breath. Usually, much sputum (the mucus you cough up) is produced by these conditions. Several illnesses can cause a distinctive breath odour. People with diabetes often have a fruity breath odour. This smell is also common in ill children who have eaten poorly for days.

Fifth, avoid fermented foods for six weeks, including cheese, alcohol, refined sugar, vinegar, sweets and chocolate; this may just tell you the cause of bad breath. Have regular dental check-ups.

Sixth, ensure regular bowel movements (once a day) by including fibre in your diet.

If the problem continues, take a breath test with your doctor to establish whether you have *Helicobacter pylori,* a bacteria that lives in the stomach and that over a period of time can cause ulcers.

Do Babies Learn Before Birth?

From the moment of birth, an infant begins rapidly absorbing information, piecing together the framework of his or her future self. But what happens during all that time the baby is still in the womb? Does learning begin in utero? Absolutely, says Rick Gilmore, Associate Professor of Psychology at Penn State University, 'There's ample evidence that fetuses are especially receptive to sounds from the mother's body and the external environment.'

He points to a hugely influential 1986 study conducted by Anthony DeCasper at the University of South Carolina that seems to prove the existence of prenatal learning. 'Mothers were instructed to read *The Cat in the Hat* out loud while they were pregnant,' Gilmore explains. 'When the babies were born, researchers tested to see if they recognized the story against other stories, and their mother's voice against other readers.'

Notes Gilmore, hearing is one of the first senses to develop. As early as 16 weeks gestation, a developing fetus begins to perceive the world outside the womb through his or her fluid-filled ears. 'Inside the womb, people's voices sound sort of muted. However there is a lot of information in that filtered and muted sound stream.'

A Japanese study shows that the fetus can also learn to ignore annoyance of ordinary life: the roar of an airplane overhead. Infants born to women who lived beneath the flight pattern of Osaka airport were five times more likely to sleep through the noise than were babies whose mothers lived elsewhere.

'It's important to understand that, while in utero learning does exist, the type of learning is quite simple,' concludes Prof. Gilmore. 'There's very little evidence of any specific thing a parent can do to affect a child's intelligence or temperament before birth.'

Get Out of the Rut

Hindu scriptures wisely tell us — 'we come empty-handed and we leave empty-handed, why then do you struggle so much'. Yet competing and striving for better status is what most of us live for. How wise is this way of living?

You don't need to make big changes to get out of a rut or to put some pizzazz back into your daily life. Sometimes you just need to fine-tune the little things in life.

Be spontaneous. One night, surprise your spouse by taking him or her out to a special dinner at the best restaurant in town. You may have to save up to do this, but that can be part of the fun.

Or, vary the way you go to work. If you drive every day but can take a public transport, use it one day and let someone else fight rush-hour traffic while you read a good book or sit back and enjoy the scenery.

The point is not to give up on life, but to stop living it insanely. Many of us are seeking happiness in the future while suffering in the present. Since we are always looking at the future, we are seldom happy in the present, no matter what it brings us.

Analyse your daily behaviour to see what repetitive patterns you've fallen into. Then make a few easy changes. You may find your life to be not only more invigorating but also more rewarding.

Escaping the rat race is the first step to sane living. Focus on what you have, rather than what you want to achieve. There is peace and a joy to life when you are not constantly worried about the next thing to achieve.

See also: GO WHERE YOU'VE NEVER GONE BEFORE; CHOOSE TO BE HAPPY.

Be Nice to Your Liver

When your body needs blood, it calls on the reserves in the liver. The amount of blood flowing to the liver is impressive; it filters 1.2 litres of blood a minute when the body is at rest. This adds up, in a year, to an enormous quantity. By one estimate, the liver filters enough blood to fill 23 milk trucks.

Weighing 1.75 kgs, (approx.) liver is the largest organ of the body and responsible for over 600 functions. It is the only organ that is bathed in blood from two sources. First, the hepatic artery from the aorta supplies the liver with fresh blood to oxygenate the cells. Second, the portal vein delivers the nutrient-rich blood from the stomach and small intestine to the liver. As this blood is filtered through the liver, nutrients are extracted, chemically processed, stored, or returned to blood circulation.

At the same time, the liver plays a role in regulating the composition of the blood. Along with the spleen, it helps to retire old red blood cells. It metabolizes a portion of the haemoglobin molecule from the used blood cells and converts it to a water-soluble form of bilirubin, a component of bile, to be excreted as a waste product.

It is the body's primary organ responsible for removing potential toxins from the blood stream; it breaks up saturated fats and oils making it possible to eliminate them. Amongst the many signs of improper liver function are intolerance to greasy and spicy food, weight gain, indigestion, chronic constipation, poor thyroid function, skin blotches, and aches and pains.

Therefore, be nice to your liver. It is life sustaining. You can't live without it.

To Nap, or Not to Nap?

'**Some of the greatest** minds and performers have been devoted nappers. Still it may seem counter intuitive and somewhat embarrassing to crawl off to a snooze while other people work,' wrote Prof. Sara C Mednick of University of California, San Diego, in *The New York Times* of September 3, 2010.

The urge for a mid-day snooze is built into your body's biological clock. This typically occurs between 1 p.m. and 4 p.m., as indicated by a slight dip in your body temperature.

Napping is not a substitute for a full night's sleep. Don't nap if sleeping at night is a problem. If you find a nap refreshes you and doesn't interfere with night time sleep, try these ideas:

Keep it short. A half-hour nap is ideal. The longer you nap, the more likely you are to feel groggy afterward. Naps longer than an hour or two are more likely to interfere with your night time sleep.

Take a mid-afternoon nap. Naps at this time produce a physically invigorating slumber.

If you can't nap, just rest. Lie down and keep your mind on something else.

After napping, be sure to give yourself time to wake up before resuming activities particularly those that require a quick or sharp response.

See also: SLEEP LIKE A BABY.

Eat Foods That Will Eventually Rot

This is a nice little rule from Michael Pollan — eat foods that will eventually rot. Follow this rule, and you will always eat fresh foods. Foods that are alive and full of nutrients. Nutrients that give you life and good health.

What does it mean for food to rot or 'go bad'? It usually means that the fungi and bacteria and creatures with which we compete for nutrients and calories have got to it before we did.

Food processing began as a way to extend the shelf life of food by protecting it from bacteria and fungi. This is often accomplished by making the food less appealing to them, by removing nutrients that attract these competitors, or by removing nutrients likely to turn rancid. The more processed a food is, the longer the shelf life, and less nutritious it typically is.

For a healthy well balanced diet make it a habit to choose unrefined whole foods such as fruits, vegetables, beans and whole grains, as opposed to refined processed foods such as soft drink, sodas, candy, cookies and cakes.

Instead of obsessing over individual ingredients, Pollan believes we should be paying attention to how our food is grown (preferably local and organically), the balance of our overall diet and advises that how we eat has as much importance as what we eat.

Real food is alive — and therefore it should eventually die. There are a few exceptions to this rule: for example, honey has a shelf life measured in centuries.

'When you pickup a packaged food, even if it is a fortified yogurt with half-a-dozen ingredients you can't pronounce, ask your self, "What are these things doing here?" says Pollan. 'Eat food,' and not 'edible food like substances,' is his advise.

Control Allergy Attacks

You can control allergic attacks of sneezing and sniffling by learning which allergens trigger an attack.

Keep a record of your attacks, noting when and where they occurred and what you were doing at the time. If you start coughing and sneezing and your eyes water when the lawn is being mowed or the leaves are being raked, come out of the lawn immediately. That will reduce your exposure to pollen from grass, trees and weeds that may be causing your problem.

You may find that you start having an allergic response in your bedroom. Keep the bedroom free of dust, moulds and other allergens. You may want to cover pillows and mattresses with plastic covers or install an air conditioner or air purifier for the room.

Whatever the season, by dusting and vacuuming frequently, by washing rugs and getting rid of objects that collect dust, you can live more comfortably.

In some people, pleasant fragrance and fresh feel of perfume also causes immediate allergic symptoms. As do some medicines, fresh paint, some cosmetics such as hair colour and skin creams. Among foods the main culprits are milk, soy, wheat, egg, peanuts and some fish, mostly shell fish.

An itchy or a runny nose, consecutive sneezing, tingling of mouth, nausea, vomit or rashes can be symptoms of a condition called as allergic rhinitis. If not treated promptly allergic rhinitis may lead to asthma and breathing difficulty.

See also: DRUG ALLERGIES; MYTHS ABOUT ALLERGY; LEARN WHAT PULLS THE ASTHMA TRIGGER; FIGHT INTOLERANCE

Cut Down on Caffeine

If you drink more than one cup of coffee a day, you could be hooked on the most widely used drug in the world: caffeine.

Caffeine takes effect in about thirty minutes and lasts from two to eight hours. It stimulates alertness chemicals in the brain, and that perks you up. But it also raises insulin levels, and that brings you down. Irritability, nervousness, insomnia and increased blood pressure can all result from 300 milligrams of caffeine — about the amount contained in three 150 ml cups of coffee or six cans of soda (cola). Energy drinks contain as much or more caffeine as most coffee.

Here are some suggestions for healthier alternatives that should keep the cravings at bay.

If you absolutely must have coffee, and because it is highly addictive, many people are unprepared for how difficult it is to go 'cold turkey'. So if you find you struggle to get through the day without at least one cup, don't despair: you can still enjoy coffee sensibly in moderation.

One good habit is drinking one similarly-sized glass of water for each mug you consume, as this will help to cancel out the dehydrating effects of the caffeine. This is a particularly good idea if you suffer from stomach cramps or headaches when you over-do the coffee.

It's also advisable to avoid drinking any caffeinated beverages after the middle of your day, as these will continue to have an effect into the evening, possibly disrupting your sleep.

Decaffeinated coffee is often frowned upon by those who really know their beans, but some varieties can be quite convincing. Chicory tastes similar to coffee, has the same taste and aroma of hot coffee but there's no caffeine at all.

Get Your Calcium the Natural Way

Calcium is necessary throughout life for strong bones and teeth and for normal heart functioning. Calcium also plays a major role in blood clotting and is vital to the healthy operation of your nervous system.

For adults, the most serious consequence of not getting enough dietary calcium is osteoporosis, a condition in which the bones become brittle and break easily. Children who don't get enough calcium will have stunted growth.

Are you concerned about getting enough calcium?

If you don't want to take dietary supplements, consider getting your calcium the old-fashioned way: through food!

Nutritional research shows that we require the following amounts of calcium at these ages:

1-11 years: 800 mg a day
11-24 years: 1,200 mg a day
25 and older: 800 mg a day

Some nutrition experts believe that post menopausal women need, 1,200-1,500 mg of calcium a day because of their greater risk of developing osteoporosis. Pregnant women may also need more to meet the demands of developing foetus.

You may want to avoid the best sources of calcium — dairy products — because of their high fat content. But skim milk, low-fat cheese and non fat yogurt have just as much calcium as their high-fat cousins.

Other foods that provide good amounts of calcium include tofu, soybeans, almonds, figs, canned salmon or sardines, broccoli, spinach and kale.

With such a wide variety of sources, you should have no difficulty getting your calcium naturally.

Forever Young

The exalted position of ***Huang Di Nei Jing*** which maybe roughly translated as *The Yellow Emperor's Classics of Internal Medicine* in traditional Chinese medicine is comparable to that in Western philosophy of Plato's *Republic.*

Since it was first written about 2600 BC, it has been regarded as most authoritative guide for the practice of traditional Chinese medicine. It is replete with ageless conclusions on longevity. One of its important messages is the relationship between moderation and longevity.

'The way to longevity involves being moderate in eating and drinking, abstinent in ejaculation, regular in living habits, calm in heart and indifferent to fame and gains, and avoiding the bad influence of extreme weather. Following these rules and the genuine qi energy will permeate the body, and your spirit will be on high alert against any disease. How can you be sick this way?

It is desirable that we reduce our earthly desires, keep the mind easy and calm, free from fear and emotional outbursts, and keep the body active but not tired.... On the contrary, to drink wine like water and engage in sexual intercourse in a drunken state; to spend the precious sexual essence freely and lead an irregular way of life, ignorant of the vital importance of semen and energy conservation — these are sure ways to get old and die prematurely.'

See also: FIGHT AGEING WITH ANTIOXIDANTS; LIVE WITH NATURE.

Contact Lenses Versus Glasses

Contact lenses are a terrific alternative to glasses. But people often find themselves in a dilemma when choosing between regular eyeglasses and contact lenses. Which is the better route to take?

Contacts allow more natural vision, and do not obscure a person's natural look. Since contacts are next to the eye, there is less distortion and every object is represented as is. The entire field of vision remains intact, whereas glasses may obscure the peripheral vision. Contact lenses are seamless, no one can know if you are wearing them or not, and this boosts the self-esteem of many individuals. Contact lenses do not mist or get wet on a rainy day, and are perfect for persons who have an active lifestyle, do a lot of driving, play sports and want to retain as much peripheral vision as is possible.

However contact lenses are not for everyone; and certainly not for anyone with dry eyes, previous corneal ulcers or corneas that have loss of sensation. Contacts are impractical for persons with arthritis, tremors and for those who simply do not have patience. With all the care necessary to use lenses, some people just get impatient.

On the other hand, there are no known problems associated with wearing glasses. Not only are they cheaper, but also easier to maintain — all you need is a clean cloth. Because of their size, glasses are less likely to get lost than contact lenses. With advancing technology, eyeglasses have become lighter, more stylish and chic.

To sum up, choose wisely and choose the option that gives best comfort and vision. But remember to have a pair of glasses as a backup in case a problem requires you to stop wearing contact lenses for a while.

Base Your Exercise on Body Type

Exercise can do wonders for your health and energy level but it can't change your body type. And your body type may make some activities easier and more effective for you. Are you an endomorph, a mesomorph or an ectomorph? Most people fall into one of these body-type categories, based on height, build, muscle tone and distribution of body fat.

In general, endomorphs are small-boned, chubby, not muscular, and broader at the hips than shoulders. Mesomorphs are usually rugged, big-boned, muscular and broad-shouldered. And ectomorphs have narrow shoulders, chests and hips, long arms and legs, and little body fat.

If you are an endomorph, you may benefit most from nonimpact or low-impact aerobic activities such as bike riding, swimming and brisk walking. Walking, running, martial arts and sports such as tennis may benefit mesomorphs the most. And for ectoporphs,

tennis, basketball, racquet sports, jogging and other similar exercises may bring the biggest aerobic benefits.

Consider using your body type as a guide when choosing how to exercise.

See also: TRY AN ANTI-AGEING PILL; AEROBIC VS ANAEROBIC EXERCISES.

Raise a Toast to Red Wine

While the news about red wine might gladden the hearts of those who enjoy a glass with their evening meal, doctors remain wary of encouraging anyone to start drinking alcohol.

Yet many doctors agree that something in red wine appears to help your heart. It's possible that antioxidants in red wine called polyphenols may help protect the lining of blood vessels in your heart. A polyphenol called resveratrol is one substance in red wine which has got much attention. It might be a key ingredient that helps to prevent damage to blood vessels, reduces 'bad' cholesterol and prevents blood clots.

The resveratrol in red wine comes from the skin of grapes used to make wine. Because red wine is fermented with grape skins longer than white wine it contains more resveratrol. Simply eating grapes, or drinking grape juice, has been suggested as one way to get resveratrol without drinking alcohol.

If you already drink red wine, do so in moderation. Moderate drinking is defined as an average of two drinks a day for men and one drink a day for women. The limit for men is higher because men generally weigh more and have more of an enzyme that metabolizes alcohol than women do. Wine, however, is not for everyone. One down side is that it can elevate triglyceride levels, which is associated with health problems like diabetes. It is often a big trigger for people who suffer with migraine headaches. People who drink alcohol also consume empty calories, calories that lack nutrients and can lead to weight gain.

150 ml red wine approx. 120 calories. Drink a bottle of wine (4 glasses), and you'll be consuming about 480 calories (equivalent of two Cokes!)

Cherish Your Friends

Studies show that from the most primitive to the most developed societies, friendship has a protective, positive effect on people. In fact, friends can even help keep each other healthy.

Over the past decade, research studies in the US performed by cognitive psychologists such as Martin E. Seligman, Ph.D., have shown that people with close friends become ill less frequently and are better able to fight disease when they do. In addition, they have more *joie de vivre* — the joy of life.

Why? No one knows for sure. But researchers at the University of Alabama have found that people who have close friendships have lower blood pressure and suffer from less heart disease and depression than people who don't. And studies at Duke University show that friends act as loving buffers against the damaging effects of stress.

An excellent way to establish friendship is to learn to be a good listener. At some time, everyone needs someone who will listen without judging and without giving unwanted advice.

A second way is to reach out and help someone without waiting to be asked. If a neighbour, or a co-worker needs help, make the first move.

A third way is to join a local group that sponsors activities you enjoy such as morning or evening walks, card games or tennis.

Cherish your friends. Reach out to others in friendship.

See also: GO WHERE YOU HAVE NEVER GONE BEFORE; CHOOSE TO BE HAPPY; FORGIVE; LEND AN EAR, OFFER A SHOULDER

Treat Your Children Well

Newborns have some natural immunity passed to them by the mother while still in the womb. However, this immunity lasts only a short time. Immunizations are critical to protect infants and children from various illnesses. Many parents do not know when their children should get recommended inoculations and when they should get booster shots.

Here is some basic information on immunizations and schedules, that parents can learn from. If your child is not protected against common childhood diseases, make an appointment with your paediatrician or a health clinic today.

Normally, after the immunization schedule is complete, children should have lifelong protection against certain diseases; however vaccines cannot always guarantee complete protection. Sometimes this is because the body may not produce enough antibodies, and immunization may need topping up and booster shots maybe needed as children get older. In the event the child does develop any of the diseases after immunization, it is likely to be in a milder form.

We should continue to use OPV (Oral Polio Vaccine) till we achieve polio eradication in India. IPV can be used additionally for individual protection.

OPV must be given to children less than 5 years of age at the time of each supplementary immunization activity.

Immunisation Schedule (upto 10 years)[1]

Age	*Vaccine*
At Birth	BCG
At Birth	OPV (1) + HEPATITIS B (1)
4 Weeks	HEPATITIS B (2)
8 Weeks	DTP (1) + OPV (2) + HIB (1)
12-14 Weeks	DTP (2) + OPV (3) + HIB (2)
18-20 Weeks	DTP (3) + OPV (4) + HIB (3)
8-9 Months	MEASLES + OPV + HEP B (3)
12-18 Months	CHICKEN-POX (Optional)
15-18 Months	MMR
15-18 Months	HIB (Booster)
18-24 Months	DTP + OPV (1st Booster)
2 Years	HEPATITIS-A VACCINE (Optional)
3 Years	TYPHOID injection
5 Years	DTP + OPV (2nd Booster)
5 Years	HEPATITIS – A (Recommended, if not given earlier)
5 Years	MMR (unless both Measles & MMR have been given)
6 Years	TYPHOID ORAL
9 Years	TYPHOID ORAL
10 Years	TETANUS
10 Years	CHICKEN POX VACCINE (Recommended, if not administered earlier / no past history of chicken-pox)

DTP Diphtheria, Tetanus, Pertussis (Whooping Cough)
OPV Oral Polio Vaccine
MMR Measles, Mumps, Rubella (German Measles)
BCG Tuberculosis Vaccine
HIB Haemophilus Influenza B Vaccine (Meningitis Vaccine)
HEP B Hepatitis B Vaccine
Varicella Vaccine Chicken Pox Vaccine

[1] Source: Indian Academy of Pediatrics

Use RICE for Strains and Sprains

Even though an injury, especially, a sports injury may require a doctor's attention, there are things you can do immediately. What you need first is RICE: Rest, Ice, Compression and Elevation.

First, sit down and rest the injured area, so you don't increase the pain and swelling or do further damage.

Second, use a bag of crushed ice to prevent or reduce swelling. Apply the ice for fifteen to twenty minutes every two hours. *Never* sleep with ice on the injury. If you have an injured foot, ankle or hand, you can immerse it in ice water (no colder than 60° F or 15.5° C) for fifteen minutes at a time rather than applying crushed ice.

Third, use an elastic wrap bandage to compress and support the injured area. Don't wrap too tightly.

And fourth, if at all possible, elevate the injured area with a pillow to help reduce swelling and ensure proper blood flow. Elevate your legs twenty-eight to thirty inches. Be on your back as much as possible.

If pain persists after forty-eight hours, see your doctor.

See also: IF YOUR ANKLE TURNS; HOW MANY KINDS OF PAIN ARE THERE?; PUT PEPPER ON YOUR PAIN.

Leave Driving to Others

According to the US National Traffic Safety Commission, 'highway hypnosis' frequently occurs on long trips during which the scenery rarely changes. You can fall into a trance from staring straight ahead at the road. You won't be able to gauge your speed, and in extreme cases, you may even begin to hallucinate.

To prevent this from happening, keep your eyes moving. Don't just look straight ahead. Regularly check your rear view mirror and your side-view mirrors. Do this even if there isn't another car in view. You can also prevent highway hypnosis by shifting your point of focus. Look up the road then shift your focus to the dashboard, then back to the road.

If your eyes burn or you realize a period of time has gone by and you can't account for it, pull over. You've had enough driving.

As hard as it may be to admit, there comes a time when a senior citizen should park his or her car for good. Accident rates sky-rocket in people over seventy-five, and those over eighty are as dangerous on the road as teenagers. What's more, according to the *Wall Street Journal,* a senior citizen is less likely to survive an accident, even when wearing a seat belt.

Ask your family physician if he or she thinks you still have the sharp eyes and quick reflexes necessary to drive.

Depending on what your physician finds, it may be fine to continue driving, or you may want to restrict your driving to daytime trips within your neighbourhood — just as you probably restricted your teenager during his accident-prone years. Or it may even be time to hang up your car keys for good.

Follow the Golden Rule

Are you harbouring a grudge or resentment toward someone? Let it go today and forgive the person. The health benefits of forgiving others — and sometimes of forgiving yourself — are significant. When you forgive a fellow human being, you gain both psychologically and physically.

Research has shown that people become more relaxed when they are forgiving. They also feel physically warmer. Breathing becomes easier, and blood pressure and heart rate lower. In addition, when you forgive another, you connect with the love that is inside you.

Forgiving is simply putting the universal Golden Rule into practice which tells us that one should treat others as one would like others to treat oneself; one should not treat others in ways that one would not like to be treated.

Who among us hasn't needed forgiveness? Forgiveness is a way you can let go of anger and pain and increase the love and joy in your life.

See also: CHERISH YOUR FRIENDS; LEND AN EAR, OFFER A SHOULDER.

Take Your Blood Pressure Twice

Blood pressure is measured using two numbers. The first measures what is called systolic pressure, meaning the pressure exerted against the walls of your arteries while your heart is beating. The second measures what is called diastolic pressure, or the pressure between heartbeats when your heart is at rest. The two numbers are recorded one over the other, as in 120/80.

You need two or more readings, taken on separate occasions, to get an accurate blood pressure measurement. Remember that blood pressure readings vary throughout the day. They usually are highest in the morning after you wake up and move around. They tend to decrease throughout the day and are lowest in the evening.

You should also have your blood pressure taken when standing, seated and lying down, since this will give your doctor a better idea of what's normal for you. Have your blood pressure checked annually. Keeping your blood pressure normal will reduce your risk of heart attack, stroke and kidney disease.

Classification of Normal and High Blood Pressure

	Systolic	Diastolic
Optimal	<120	<80
Normal	<130	<85
High-Normal	130-139	85-89
Hypertension:		
Stage 1	140-159	90-99
Stage 2	>160	>100

US Joint National Committee (JNC) on Detection, Evaluation and Treatment of High Blood Pressure, 7th Report, 2004

Tense Your Muscles to Relax

Progressive Muscle Relaxation (PMR) developed in the 1930s by Edmund Jacobason, is a great way to release tension. With PMR, you work with four muscle groups.

Group 1 Forearms and biceps
Group 2 Feet, calves, thighs and buttocks
Group 3 Chest, stomach and lower back
Group 4 Shoulders, neck, throat, face and head

To see how effective PMR can be, sit in a comfortable chair or lie down on a comfortable bed or sofa. Breathe deeply and slowly. Then when you feel relaxed, tense the first muscle group. Hold the muscles tense for about ten seconds. You may feel a slight burning sensation. Let the muscles go limp and relax. Repeat this procedure twice. Work on the first muscle group for two or three days, then move to the second muscle group, the third and finally the fourth.

Experiment with PMR and find out what works best for you. Go slowly. Don't tense any muscle group so much that it hurts.

See also: EXERCISE YOUR 'MUSCLE OF LOVE'; THE RIGHT WAY TO STRETCH; GIVE YOURSELF A HELPING HAND.

Women: Check Your Breasts

Women should begin monthly breast self-examination at age twenty and continue it throughout life, experts suggest. Eighty per cent of cancerous tumours are discovered by women themselves.

How should the breasts be examined? At first, you may want to examine them daily to get used to how your breasts normally feel. Over time, you'll be able to notice changes.

The monthly breast self-examination is best carried out in the morning, a few days after your period.

The first part should be done in the shower. When you get in the shower, raise one arm and, with fingers held flat, gently feel about your breast for lumps or thickening. Use your right hand to examine your left breast and your left hand to examine your right breast.

Second part of self-examination should be done in the bed. Lie down, place a pillow under your right shoulder and put your right hand behind your head. Starting at the outermost top edge of your right breast, slowly move your flat fingers in spiralling motion towards the nipple, examining the whole breast. Feel for lumps from under your armpit all the way to your collarbone. Repeat this procedure with your left breast.

The third part of the self-examination should be in front of a mirror. Stand in front of a mirror with your arms at your sides. Look for puckering or dimpling and changes in breast size, colouring and texture. Raise your arms above your head and look again. Then gently squeeze the nipples and look for any discharge.

At the slightest indication of change seek an evaluation from your physician/gynaecologist.

Try an Anti-ageing 'Pill'

Exercise is probably the world's greatest medicine. It reduces stress, anxiety and depression and can help prevent heart disease and other illnesses. The U.S. National Institute on Ageing notes that 'if exercise could be packed in a pill, it would be the single most widely prescribed and beneficial medicine in the world.' In fact, regular exercise may prevent most age-related physical deterioration.

Researchers at the University of Florida Center for Exercise Sciences have studied the anti-ageing effects of exercise. And they have found that seniors benefit from regular exercise more than any other age group. In fact, even men and women in their 90s achieve great benefits from beginning regular exercise.

It wasn't that long ago. Scientist believed that a substantial loss of strength was an inevitable part of ageing. After all, some decrease in muscle mass is a normal part of getting older. But it's now clear that if you're dedicated to maintaining your strength, you can make great strides in doing so as you age.

Studies have shown that strength can be maintained and perhaps increased at any age — even in your 80s and beyond. The key is to dedicate yourself to a regular and progressive program of strength exercises.

In one study, people in their late 80s and early 90s performed regular strength training exercises over a 12-week period. The results showed an increase in the strength of the participants' upper thigh (quadriceps) muscles by an average of 175 per cent. They also improved their balance and found climbing stairs to be easier.

No matter how old or young you are, it's never too late or too soon to begin exercising.

See also: BASE YOUR EXERCISE ON BODY TYPE.

Educate Yourself on Mammography

There is some disagreement among doctors over when a woman should first have a mammogram. Some recommend a 'baseline' mammogram at age thirty-five, followed by yearly mammography beginning at age forty. Other doctors think that women don't need mammography until age fifty.

One thing that everyone agrees on, however, is that mammography is both essential and critical and that a good clinical analysis is as important as competent imaging.

To ensure the best 'pictures' possible, don't use a deodorant or talcum powder on the day of your mammogram.

The talc in the powder and the aluminium hydroxide in the deodorant are absorbed through the skin in the underarm area. These materials can then pass into breast tissue and possibly show up on the mammogram as calcium deposits.

Calcium deposits in breast tissue are one of the signs indicating that cancer is present. So by using talcum powder or a deodorant before your test, you could create the conditions that would result in a false-positive test result. In other words, your mammogram would indicate cancer where there is none.

Don't worry about perspiration on the day of your exam. You can take care of that after you have had your mammogram.

See also: WOMEN: CHECK YOUR BREASTS; BREAST TENDERNESS.

Clean Out Your Medicine Cabinet

When was the last time you cleaned out your medicine cabinet? It has been quite a while, isn't it? Your medicine cabinet is not meant to be a storage area for all the medicines that you or any one in the family has ever been prescribed. For whatever reason, we often have leftover or half-used prescriptions in the medicine cabinet.

In general, you usually shouldn't have any leftover prescription medicine after you have finished treatment for an illness, even for an ear infection or a sore throat. If you do have left-over medicines, then you probably bought more than the doctor prescribed or did not complete the prescribed course. Either way, not a good idea.

Take the time to go through your medicine cabinet and get rid of prescription medications that are over one year old. Check the expiration dates on any over-the-counter products and throw out the ones that have expired. Then take any remaining medications and move them to a drawer or cabinet in another room. Medications can deteriorate in the heat and dampness of the bathroom.

It is best to get rid of any medicines that haven't been stored properly and any empty prescription bottles.

Once you have decided which medicines to get rid of, you should have a plan on what to do with them. Almost everything in your medicine cabinet, including sunscreen and over-the-counter medications, have expiration dates, and should be replaced once they are outdated.

Should you throw them in the trash or simply flush them down the toilet? No way! Ask you doctor or the nearest hospital for safe hazardous waste disposal options. Kids can get to medicines you throw into the garbage, and medicines you flush will end up in our ground water.

In addition to old medications, make sure you are keeping your children safe and this may mean getting rid of mercury thermometer and baby aspirin.

Mercury thermometers can break, exposing your child to the mercury and mercury vapours; instead opt for the safer digital thermometers which can be used in the mouth or under the armpit or ear or forehead.

You only have to get rid of aspirin or baby aspirin if it's part of your child's medicine cabinet. Remember that because of the risk of Reye's syndrome, you shouldn't usually give your child, or even your teenager, aspirin.

And don't forget: Make sure that children cannot reach the place where medicines are stored.

Don't Apologize for Eating Beans

Beans are an excellent source of plant protein, contain no saturated fat or cholesterol and provide nutrients such as iron, potassium, folic acid and zinc. Despite being tasty and nutritious some people avoid eating beans because they cause gas. The severity and frequency of flatulence associated with consuming beans can be reduced by soaking them.

Soaking beans and other legumes in water for twelve hours before cooking them can limit their gaseous side effects — an integral part of Indian cooking tradition — has now been confirmed by researchers.

Soaking the beans before cooking reduces the sugar content of the beans by up to 30 per cent — it's the sugar that causes flatulence. Boiling is more effective than using a pressure cooker in reducing gas from kidney beans, while lentils do better in a pressure cooker. Chickpeas and kidney beans that are kept in their cooking water for five hours at a temperature of 95° F or 35° C had even less sugar.

Beans play an important role in reducing your risk of colon cancer and heart disease, but not everyone needs to know when you've eaten them!

See also: FLATULENCE: TREATMENT AND PREVENTION; LOVEABLE LEGUMES; PAY ATTENTION TO YOUR BODY'S SIGNALS; MAGIC OF SPROUTS.

Talk about Sex

Couples who have been together for decades say that all it takes to keep love alive is a little effort.

In the past, it was falsely believed that seniors have no interest in sex, except for a few 'dirty old men.' A more current myth is that seniors are (or should be) highly sexually active.

Actually, your sexuality is in a constant state of change. As men get older, some take longer to achieve erection and orgasm. And some women experience a gradual decrease in sexual desire, while others become more sexually responsive. Menopause symptoms, illness and the normal effects of ageing all contribute to your changing sexuality.

Surveys show that among seniors, sexual activity is more common than abstinence. And many married people over age sixty-five (even some in their eighties and nineties) still have sex regularly.

According to Robert N. Butler, MD, of Mount Sinai Medical Center in New York City, some people go to bed together, hold each other in their arms and fall in love all over again.

You may find that 'rituals' help recapture special feelings. Return regularly to a place that played an important role in your love, such as the spot where you decided to marry or where you spent your honeymoon.

If you're experiencing sexual problems, talk to your doctor no matter what age you are. Whether your problem has a physical or an emotional cause, a few tips from your doctor may help you enjoy a satisfying sexual life.

The greatest pleasure in learning the secrets of lasting love is the process of learning itself.

See also: MAKE LOVE AFTER HEART ATTACK.

Lose Weight Gradually

If you're trying to lose weight, do so gradually and you're more likely to keep it off.

Try to lose a quarter to half kilo a week, or one to one and a half kilos in a month. Aim to attain a healthy weight a year from now, not next week.

Setting small, achievable goals for yourself will also keep you away from the crash diets and fad diets that inevitably lead to failure. Success breeds success, and you may soon achieve a weight goal that has eluded you for a long time.

You must first realize how much food you are eating. Look at how much you put on your plate and ask yourself if you are really full after each meal. If you are miserable after you eat because you are eating too much, then that is an obvious sign that you should eat smaller portions. You should not feel full after every meal, but you should feel content and no longer hungry. Once you have a good idea of how much you normally eat, begin to cut down on that amount, but only by a little bit.

Many people make the mistake of starving themselves when they want to lose weight. This only causes you to be very hungry, so that when you eat later, you eat even more than normal. Also, if you completely starve yourself, your body will go into defence mode and store the fat in your body for later because it believes you do not have enough food. When you first cut down on your food amount, you only need to cut down a spoonful at a time. Gradually increase the amount of food that you are cutting down. One thing that helps some people is to begin eating off of a smaller plate. A full small plate looks like more food than a few piles of food on a big plate. Once you are accustomed to eating a smaller amount, try to begin eating a little healthier. Again, if you totally cut all of the foods you love from your diet, you will crave them and overeat when you have the chance to eat them. Begin eating more of the healthy foods that you do like, and try to learn to like the ones that you don't. Try to bake some of your foods that are usually fried.

Always check the ingredients, calories, fat, carbohydrates, and vitamins of the food you buy. Food with a lot of vitamins will give you more energy and will not make you hungry, unlike foods that are all sugar. Keep an eye on your calorie, fat, and carbohydrate intake, but don't become a counter. Remember, you are on your own diet, losing weight at your own pace. Do not get frustrated if you do not see results immediately. The goal is to lose weight gradually. When you lose weight gradually, you keep it off. Dropping two kilos in one day is not healthy, and it will not stay off. Just be patient, keep working, and always remind yourself that you want to be healthier and that you want to have a better body. If you have no motivation, it will be much harder to succeed.

If you have access to exercise equipment, use it. Walk on a treadmill, starting at ten minutes each time. Walking on a treadmill will not do much for your body, but walking for any length of time without stopping increases your endurance and this will help you when you decide to try more difficult exercise, such as jogging and running outside in the heat.

Also, do some crunches. Do not put your hands behind your neck because that will put unnecessary strain on your back. Do not sit all the way up, just do crunches. Remember your goal is to lose weight, but to go all the way you need to be healthier all around.

See also: AVOID 'GUARANTEED' WEIGHT LOSS PLAN; UNEXPECTED WEIGHT CHANGES.

Take Snoring Seriously

If your partner's snoring ruins your sleep, the answer may not be separate bedrooms. Your partner may need to see a doctor. Snoring may signal a life-threatening condition.

People who snore loudly may suffer from obstructive sleep apnea, a condition in which breathing is disrupted during sleep for short periods. Sleep apnea can be caused by enlarged tonsils or adenoids or by a disturbance of the central nervous system.

You need to take this condition seriously, because sleep apnea can sometimes bring on a stroke or heart attack.

Most people with sleep apnea are overweight. Weight loss helps some people but not everyone. Thin people snore too. Alcohol and sedatives can make the condition worse. They reduce the resting tone of the muscles at the back of the throat increasing the likelihood of snoring. People who don't normally snore will snore after drinking alcohol.

Allergens in the bedroom or in the pillow may contribute to snoring. When did you last dust the ceiling fan? Replace your pillow? If you feel fine during the day but obstructed at night, these may just be the causes.

Keeping the nasal passages open are also helpful. Rinsing your nose with salt water helps to keep the nasal passages open.

If someone has told you that you snore loudly, see your doctor. You don't want to take this problem lightly.

See also: SLEEP LIKE A BABY.

Fight Intolerance

People who are lactose-intolerant are unable to digest milk and milk products. Gas, diarrhoea, abdominal cramps, bloating and other uncomfortable symptoms can appear within a few hours of drinking milk or eating milk products.

Many people outgrow their need for milk and milk products, and their bodies develop a deficiency in the enzyme needed to digest milk. This problem is more common among women because they drink more milk than men to keep their calcium levels high.

Lactose intolerance is not an all-or-nothing thing. If you're lactose-intolerant, you can still have small amounts of milk. Some people find that by gradually increasing the amount of milk or milk-containing products in their diet they are able to better tolerate lactose without developing symptoms. And even if you're highly sensitive, you can add Lactaid (sold in liquid and tablet forms) to milk, which will provide the missing enzyme. Or you can drink soy milk or milk already treated with lactose.

See also: CONTROL ALLERGY ATTACKS; MYTHS ABOUT ALLERGY.

The Multi-talented Vitamin C

Vitamin C is probably the best known and most widely used of the vitamins. It was first discovered when Jacques Cartier (1491-1557), a French explorer who opened up Newfoundland and Canada, connected the absence of fresh fruit and vegetables to scurvy.

Ascorbic acid, a synthetic form of vitamin C, does not appear in nature, and is thus synthetically made.

Literature on vitamin C is extensive; it is needed by the body to form the collagen in bones, cartilage, muscle, blood vessels and aids in the absorption of iron. Patients with scurvy are treated with vitamin C.

It has been claimed to have a therapeutic effect on everything from colds to cancer. The use of vitamin C in the prevention and treatment of common cold and respiratory infection is a subject of on-going research. According to Mayo Clinic, 'In people who develop cold while taking vitamin C, no difference in severity of symptoms has been seen overall, although a small, significant reduction in the duration of colds has been reported.'

Vitamin C prevents the destruction of B vitamins, helps your body absorb iron and enables your body to fight infections. It also helps wounds heal and assists your body in making collagen, which holds the cells together. It may also reduce cholesterol and help prevent cancer.

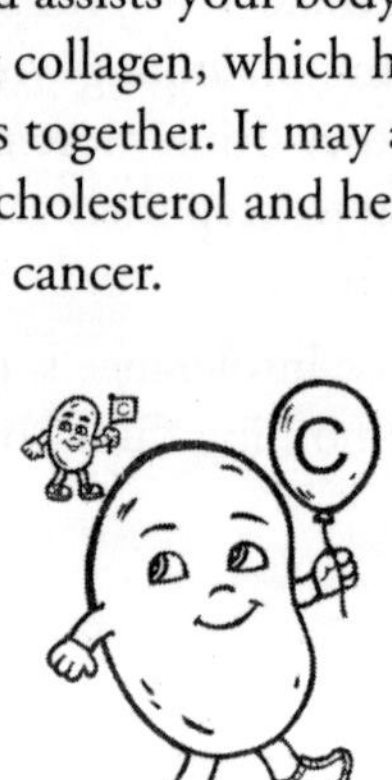

Vitamin C cannot be stored in the body; tests on animals deprived of vitamin C begin to show signs of deficiency within two weeks. Deficiency signs in humans include swelling and tenderness of the joints, appearance of nodules on the rib cage at the juncture with the sternum, bleeding of gums or loosening of teeth, slow healing of wounds, and inability to metabolize amino acids. A daily supply of vitamin C is recommended.

You can get vitamin C from oranges and other citrus fruits and their juices. Other good sources include cantaloupe, strawberries, brussels sprouts, broccoli, green peppers, asparagus, cauliflower and tomatoes.

Vitamin C is soluble in water and insoluble in oil; thus vitamin tablets should be taken with water to be assimilated. It is destroyed by alkalies, and by drying of the fruits or vegetables containing the vitamin. Freezing however, has no effect on it.

Requirements for vitamin C are felt to increase during pregnancy, infectious diseases, gastrointestinal problems, endocrine disturbances, and malignancies.

Since each person's requirements are different, a 'threshold test' has been developed which measures the vitamin C 'spilling over' into the urine.

The minimum daily requirement established for vitamin C is 30 milligrams per day, although some physicians recommend doses of up to 1,000 milligrams and even higher for specific diseases and therapeutic diets.

It is estimated that each cigarette smoked burns up 25 milligrams of vitamin C.

See also: NEVER MIX ASPIRIN WITH VITAMIN C; A CURE FOR COMMON COLD.

Live with Nature

Hu Shicong (1095-1183), who for more than four decades was doctor to Ghengis Khan's family of the Yuan dynasty, summarized his understanding of the secrets of rejuvenation and longevity in his book *Essentials of Diet:*

'In ancient times, people who understood Tao lived in harmony with Nature. They were careful in their diet, regular in their living, and moderate in work and exercise. Hence, they enjoyed long life. Nowadays, however, people behave in a quite different manner. They lead an irregular life, and are indiscriminating in diet. It is little wonder that many of them just get old before fifty.

In spring, go to bed early and rise early in harmony with the sun. Meanwhile, as the weather starts to get warm, take more wheat products to slightly cool down the qi.

In summer, the heavenly qi and the earthly qi merge. It is important that you go to bed late in the evening but get up early in the morning. Do not feel tired of the long summer day, but keep a calm, happy mind. Meanwhile, eat plenty of foods that are cool in nature.

In autumn, the heavenly qi is moving fast and the earthly qi is clear. During this time, you should go to bed early and get up early. Meanwhile, conserve your spirit and qi energy. Since autumn is a dry season, it is advisable to eat plenty of juicy foods.

In winter, the earth is frozen. This is a closing and saving season. During this time of the year, you should go to bed early in the evening but get up late in the morning after the sun is out. This is the way to conserve your energy and avoid external affections. Meanwhile, eat more foods that are warm and hot in nature. This is the way to health and longevity.'

Eat for Your Teeth

Tooth decay is the primary cause of toothache. Bacteria in the mouth thrive on the sugar and starch in food. These bacteria form a sticky plaque that clings to the surface of teeth. Acids produced by the bacteria in plaque can eat through tooth enamel, creating a cavity. The first sign of decay may be a sensation of pain, when one eats something very sweet, very cold or very hot.

Until you can see the dentist, try self-care tips: rinse the mouth with warm water; use dental floss to remove any food particles wedged between teeth or take an over-the-counter pain reliever.

The direct application of clove oil also helps ease toothache.

Nutritional research shows that a balanced diet of dairy products, poultry, fish, vegetables, fruits and whole grains is essential for healthy teeth and gums.

What's more, eating raw, crunchy vegetables stimulates your gums and helps clean your teeth. Extra dose of vitamin C from citrus fruits such as lemons, oranges and sweet lime also helps prevent the staining of the tooth enamel. That's why some dentists call vegetables such as broccoli and cauliflower detergent vegetables.

Next time you go food shopping, make sure these 'detergents' are on your list. What you eat — and what you don't eat — can affect whether you keep or lose your teeth as you age.

See also: TOOTH DECAY AND TOOTH ACHES; BE A HEALTHY SHOPPER.

Protect Your Vocal Cords

Most of us don't think about our vocal cords until we develop laryngitis or become hoarse. But like any other tissue, your vocal cords can become strained through overuse.

Many things we do can injure our vocal cords. Talking too much, screaming, constantly clearing your throat or smoking can make you hoarse. These can also lead to other more serious problems of the vocal cords.

You can help protect your voice by keeping the air in your home from getting too dry. Also, make sure to drink eight to ten glasses of water each day, and your vocal cords will get the lubrication they need.

Speak softly if you need to be on the telephone for long periods of time. Use a headset or phone rest, too. Muscle tension in the face, neck and throat can increase tension in the vocal cords. And try not to speak in a tone of voice that is higher or lower than your normal pitch. This causes strain.

If you become hoarse despite these precautions, don't whisper. Whispering requires more effort than speaking softly. And avoid speaking at all unless you absolutely must.

See also: GRANDMA KNOWS BEST.

Move Fast When Poison is Involved

Don't panic but get moving if you think you or a member of your household has swallowed something poisonous, gotten poisonous material in the eyes or absorbed by the skin, or inhaled poisonous fumes or vapours.

Call your doctor or local hospital. Explain what happened as simply and clearly as you can. If possible, identify the poison.

You can handle most cases of poisoning at home. But you must remain calm, so you can listen to the instructions you receive on the phone and follow them exactly.

Under no circumstances should you ever induce vomiting if a person is unconscious or drowsy, as this can obstruct the airway. According to Mayo Clinic ipecac syrup should not be given to the person suspected to have swallowed poison as it can do more harm than good.

In case a person has swallowed poison remove anything remaining in the person's mouth. Unless the victim is unconscious having a seizure, or cannot swallow give about 50 ml of water to drink.

If a person has gotten poisonous material in the eye gently flush the eye for 10 minutes using slightly warm water. Pour a stream of water from a clean glass held about 3 inches above the eye.

In case of poison on the skin remove any contaminated clothing. Rinse the skin with large amounts of water for 10 minutes. And if somebody has inhaled poison get to fresh air as soon as possible. Avoid breathing the fumes.

Many conditions mimic the symptoms of poisoning, including seizures, stroke and insulin reactions. If there is no indication of poisoning, do not treat the person for poisoning but rush to the nearest hospital.

The Gentle Way to Get Rid of Acne

Acne is a skin condition that occurs when your hair follicles become plugged with oil and dead skin cells. It most commonly appears on the face, neck, chest, back and shoulders. It can be distressing and annoyingly persistent. Acne heals slowly, and when one begins to resolve, others seem to crop up.

Contrary to popular opinion, you don't get acne from eating oily foods. You get it from increased amounts of male sex hormones called androgens. These hormones, which naturally increase during puberty in men and during pregnancy in women, stimulate the production of sebum, an oily substance that can become trapped in the hair follicles on the skin. If too much sebum is produced, acne can result. Men have more and worse acne than women because they have more androgens.

The best thing you can do is gently wash your skin twice a day. But too much washing can irritate the skin. The affected areas should be washed with a gentle cleanser which is oil free and water based. Antiseptic creams and lotions that contain benzoyl peroxide can help dry up pimples.

When using cosmetics it is best to go for powder cosmetics rather than cream products because they are less irritating. All make up should be removed before going to bed.

And finally, never pick or squeeze pimples.

Pat, Purr and Play with Your Pet

They help relieve pain, reduce tension, lower blood pressure and combat depression. They are recommended by many doctors and psychologists. And they are not a new class of wonder drugs. They are *pets.*

Researchers are documenting the great health benefits that pets bring to their owners. Dogs and cats top the list of favourite pets, but fish, birds, hamsters and many other animals can do the trick just as well. At the University of Pennsylvania, Aaron Katcher, Ph.D., and his colleagues have shown that pets do wonders for their owners. According to Centre for Disease Control and Prevention, USA, Pets can decrease blood pressure, cholesterol levels, triglyceride levels, feelings of loneliness of their owners. Pets can increase opportunities for exercises and outdoor activities and opportunities for socialization for their owner's.

Remember, not all pets are for everyone — but you may find that the benefits of owning a pet far outweigh the burdens of responsibility.

See also: TAKE IT EASY; STAY CALM AND LIVE LONGER.

Lend an Ear, Offer a Shoulder

When someone is recently bereaved, he often needs to express his feelings to get relief from his pain. And to help, all you have to do is to listen.

While you can't take away the pain of the loss, you can provide much-needed comfort and support. There are many ways to help a grieving friend or family member, starting with letting the person know you care. The bereaved struggle with many intense and frightening emotions, including depression, anger and guilt. You might not know exactly what to say or what to do, but that's okay. You don't need to have answers or give advice. The most important thing you can do is to simply be there.

Most bereavement counsellors recommend that you let the bereaved do the talking. Just your being there — to hold hands or give a hug — helps him heal. Sometimes you won't say anything. You may just cry when the bereaved person cries.

You can also help volunteering to do small chores around the house or to go shopping or do other errands. Remember to invite the bereaved person to come over to your place or to go out for a meal in the weeks and months after his loss.

As time goes on, family and friends return to their normal routines. This is when you can really be there for someone who has lost a loved one.

Limit Your Exposure to X Rays

X rays are a wonderful addition to the world of medicine. They allow the doctor to peer inside the body without opening it up. But X rays can also be harmful; according to Dr. John Gofman, Ph.D., professor emeritus at the University of California, Berkeley, we tend receive too many.

You may not think twice when a doctor or a dentist tells you that you need an X ray. Ask why you need it and if it is absolutely necessary. Sometimes X rays are ordered for legal, not medical, reasons, and you may want to refuse them. If you are seeing a doctor for a second opinion, take the X ray from the first physician with you. If you change dentists or are going for an examination by a dental specialist, take your X rays with you.

The harmful effects of X ray include many things. Being a kind of high energy radiation it can be destructive to all living tissues, including bone marrow. They are particularly harmful for pregnant women and are known to cause birth defects or congenital disorders.

However it is important to keep these risks in perspective and compare them with the benefit of doctors being able to keep on eye on the insides without surgery.

Nevertheless, always ask for X-ray shields or lead aprons for the parts of your body not being X-rayed.

Exercise Your 'Muscle of Love'

Yes, there is a 'love muscle.' It's called the pubococcygeal muscle, and there is an exercise that can help both men and women strengthen it and enhance their sex lives.

According to a researcher at Loyola University of Chicago Stritch School of Medicine, the Kegel exercise strengthens the 'love muscle' and allows men to make love longer by preventing premature ejaculating. In women, the exercise apparently produces more satisfying orgasms.

In both men and women, the pubococcygeal muscle controls urination. You can strengthen this muscle by Kegel exercise which consists of repeatedly contracting as if you were preventing urination and relaxing the muscles that form the pelvic floor. Each morning, contract this muscle thirty-six times, then rest for two minutes. Contract the muscle another thirty-six times, then rest for another two minutes. Do this for ten minutes.

You can expect to see results after several weeks.

See also: TALK ABOUT SEX; MAKE LOVE AFTER A HEART ATTACK.

Men: Add Tomatoes to Your Diet

If you're a man, add tomatoes and tomato-based foods to your diet today. They can help protect you from prostate cancer according to Mayo Clinic.

Researchers at the Harvard School of Public Health recently studied the eating habits of 47,000 men and found that those who ate at least ten servings of tomatoes and tomato-based foods each week had a 45 per cent reduction in the rate of prostate cancer. Men who ate four to seven servings of tomatoes and tomato-based foods each week had a 20 per cent reduction in the rate of prostate cancer.

Why? Researchers don't know. They do know, however, that tomatoes are rich in the antioxidant lycopene and that tomatoes proved beneficial when eaten raw, in sauces, as juice and even cooked with other vegetables. The researchers recommend that you eat a variety of vegetables and aim for ten servings of tomatoes a week as part of your overall healthy diet.

See also: LEARN CANCER'S WARNING SIGNS; ARE MALES MORE AGGRESSIVE THAN FEMALES; THE PAIN OF MALE MENOPAUSE.

Crushing Chest Pressure

Despite all the exhortations in recent years to take possible signs of heart attack seriously, a study in the *Journal of the American Medical Association* showed that 40 to 50 per cent of those with symptoms still ignore them for up to six hours. Unfortunately, heart muscle begins to die within 30 minutes of the onset of an attack, according to interventional cardiologist Dr. David Fischman, at Jefferson Medical College in Philadelphia, USA.

Especially shocking is a recent study by researchers at New York-Presbyterian Hospital which found that half the women surveyed would not call for help even if they thought they were having a heart attack.

Part of the problem is that people expect a heart attack to hurt, yet the most dangerous symptom is not pain but pressure, according to Dr Fischman. 'Sharp pain is more likely to be musculoskeletal — annoying but not dangerous,' he says. 'What you have to be careful of is sudden chest discomfort that feels like someone is sitting on your chest. The feeling of pressure can also radiate into your arms, back, and jaw. If moving around or pushing down on your chest makes it worse, it's probably not a heart attack; if it's the same when you move, you need to be evaluated immediately.'

Women need to be especially careful, says Dr Fischman: 'They're less likely to feel chest pressure and more likely to have easily overlooked discomfort in the arm, back, or jaw. It's crucial that you be aware of your body. If the feeling isn't the norm for you, get it checked out.'

Call your doctor immediately — or, better yet, make the call while you're on the way to the hospital. 'And it couldn't hurt,' says Dr Fischman, 'to pop an aspirin on the way.'

The Worst Headache of Your Life

We all have headaches, but in some cases, a pain in the head can be a sign of a life-threatening medical emergency, like a ruptured aneurysm or a stroke.

According to experts at Mayo Clinic, if you experience a 'sudden severe headache like a clap of thunder,' especially if it gets worse despite resting and taking standard over-the-counter pain medicine, it might mean that an aneurysm — a weakness in the wall of a blood vessel — had ruptured, causing bleeding into the brain.

That's as bad as it sounds and requires immediate medical attention. A headache that's accompanied by slurred speech or weakness on one side of your body is a classic sign of a stroke, most often caused by a blockage in the brain's blood supply. You have a 'golden window' of just a few hours in which treatment is most effective — get to a hospital as soon as possible.

If a worsening headache follows even a minor fall or blow to the head, it can be a tip-off to potentially lethal brain swelling. Call your doctor immediately regardless of the time of day.

See also: HOW MANY KINDS OF PAIN ARE THERE; WHEN YOU SHOULDN'T WAIT AND SEE.

Learn what Pulls the Asthma Trigger

'**Bronchial asthma is** a common condition which affects roughly one per·cent of the world population,' says Prof. Dr. O.P. Jaggi, former Dean of the faculty of Medical Sciences, University of Delhi, and Director of V. Patel Chest Institute, Delhi. It's a physical illness, although an internal chemical cascade triggered by strong emotion can also cause an attack. Its incidence is a little more in boys than in girls; this difference disappears in adult life.

A trigger is something that causes airways to narrow, leading to asthma symptoms. Everyone's asthma is different, and everyone has different triggers. For most people with asthma, triggers are only a problem when their asthma is not well-controlled.

In an asthma attack, muscle spasms in the lungs' air passages cause the airways to narrow making it more difficult to move air in and out of their lungs. The result is wheezing, coughing chest tightness and breathing difficulties associated with an asthma attack.

In many people allergies can trigger asthma symptoms. Asthma attacks are frequently brought on by breathing

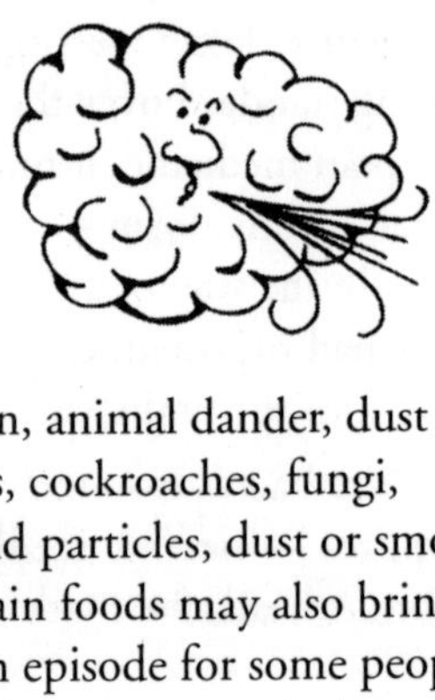

pollen, animal dander, dust mites, cockroaches, fungi, mould particles, dust or smoke. Certain foods may also bring on an episode for some people, and drugs — prescription and over-the-counter — contain ingredients to which some people are allergic. Even exercise has been known to cause an asthmatic episode.

Asthma occurs more often in persons who have a family

history of disease. The greater the degree of inheritance, the greater the likelihood of the child becoming sensitive. One inherits an allergic predisposition rather than a specific allergic disease; children of a parent suffering from hay fever may develop asthma or eczema and not necessarily hay fever.

Childhood infections, such as measles, pneumonia, whooping cough or infection in the tonsils and adenoids can set up symptoms of asthma in an already predisposed child.

Any excessive emotional reaction is sometimes known to precipitate asthma in a person who is already predisposed to it.

Generally speaking, a dry climate is better suited to an asthmatic than a humid one; he feels better away from a sea coast than near it. A dry climate, however, is no panacea for the asthmatic, as there are many other factors that come into the picture. Rainy weather, with its increased humidity, is troublesome to some asthmatics. But people who are allergic to pollens feel better after the rain, as all the pollens present in the air get washed down.

Some occupations are particularly hazardous for people with asthma. Farmers, poultry-men, dairy workers and bakers are exposed to a large number of pollens; upholsterers and mattress renovators are exposed to large quantities of house dust; flour-mill workers and carpenters are exposed to various kinds of dust. For asthmatics such occupations may lead to an aggravation of the symptoms.

Since asthma is a chronic disease; it requires ongoing treatment. Keep a record of asthma attacks and the circumstances surrounding them. You may be able to identify asthma triggers and eliminate them from your life.

The right care can make the difference between suffering with an allergic disease and feeling better.

See also: CONTROL ALLERGY ATTACKS; MYTHS ABOUT ALLERGY; DRUG ALLERGIES.

Men: Check Your Testicles

Testicular self-examination saves lives. That's because although testicular cancer is common in men between fifteen and thirty-five years of age, the cure rate is very high — 95 to 97 per cent — when the cancer is detected early.

Men under age thirty-five should examine their testes once a month. After a warm bath or shower, when the skin around the scrotum is relaxed, gently roll each testicle in both hands.

Each testicle should feel firm, but not rock hard. One testicle may be lower or slightly larger than the other. If you find a small, hard lump (like a pea), have an enlarged testicle, or notice any other differences, see your doctor as soon as you can. A lump on the testicle is often the first sign of testicular cancer and it is very much possible to determine if it is benign. Keep in mind that some cases of testicular cancer do not show symptoms until they reach an advanced stage and most testicular cancers are treatable.

Sudden, severe (acute) pain in the scrotum or testicle that lasts for more than a few minutes is an emergency. If you have this type of pain, seek immediate medical attention.

Always talk to your doctor if you have any doubts or questions.

See also: MEN: ADD TOMATOES TO YOUR DIET; LEARN CANCER'S WARNING SIGNS.

If Your Ankle Turns

When you sprain your ankle, you stretch one or more of the three main ligaments that hold the joint together. If you don't treat the sprain properly, the fibres in these ligaments can heal in an inappropriately shortened or lengthened position, leaving you prone to further injury. Indeed, up to 30 per cent of people who sprain their ankles develop 'chronic ankle instability,' leading to a cycle of repeated injury.

If you turn your ankle and can't walk on it at all — or even put weight on it — go to the emergency room to rule out severe ligament damage and broken bones. If you can walk without excruciating pain, wrap your ankle with a compression bandage to reduce swelling, and get off your feet. Keep your ankle elevated as much as possible for 48 hours, applying ice for 20 minutes every two hours.

'Even after the pain and swelling are gone, don't consider yourself fully healed,' says surgeon Dr John Kennedy, of the Hospital for Special Surgery in New York; 'to make sure you don't reinjure your ankle, you need to strengthen it.' Kennedy recommends a regimen of balance-improving exercises, including this one:

Stand flat on one foot, with the opposite leg bent at the knee, then switch legs and repeat. Begin by brushing your teeth while standing flamingo-style for 30 seconds; work up to 3 minutes per leg.

This should strengthen your ankle and hopefully prevent any future injury.

See also: USE RICE FOR STRAINS AND SPRAINS.

A Cure for the Common Cold?

Regular work out, even moderate, not only helps tone your body and build muscle — it could also help you avoid catching cold, suggest recent studies.

'People who exercise five or more times a week get fewer and less severe colds than those who work out less often and less regularly,' says Dr David C. Nieman, director of Human Performance Laboratory at Appalachain State University in N. Carolina, USA. This study was published in online *British Medical Journal* in November 2010.

Researchers tracked the respiratory health of 1000 individuals for 12 weeks and collected information on how often they exercised and how fit they felt. They found that people who felt the fittest had 41 per cent less severe cold symptoms as compared to those who fell least fit. The duration of cold symptoms was almost 50 per cent shorter in people who worked out five or more times a week than those worked out once a week or never.

During moderate exercise, immune cells circulate more quickly through the body and are better at destroying viruses and bacteria.

Based on the current knowledge, a good immune function can be maintained by balanced diet, keeping stress to minimum, avoiding chronic fatigue and adequate sleep. A low caloric intake and quick weight reduction in a short span of time can suppress immunity. Ageing and smoking have also been associated with increased risk of infection.

See also: THE MULTI-TALENTED VITAMIN C; AAACHOO! IS IT A COLD OR THE FLU; USE ANTIBIOTICS ONLY FOR BACTERIAL INFECTIONS.

Pay Attention to Your Body's Signals

Constipation is a common condition that can affect people of all ages. It means not passing stools as often as one normally does, having to strain more than usual or being unable to completely empty the bowels.

If bowels do not regularly push the waste out, the entire digestive system can become unhealthy. Waste stays in the body longer, becomes sticky and hardens along the intestinal wall, starts to fester and enlarge intestinal pores, letting toxins into the blood stream.

Through the bloodstream these harmful substances are carried throughout the body, lowering the immunity, promoting over growth of candida, a fungus causing nervousness, depression, skin disorders, headaches, fatigue, muscle weakness and an endless list of illnesses.

If you're eating a healthy diet — with lots of fresh fruits and vegetables and whole grains — but still experience constipation, it may be your behaviour that's causing the problem.

Everyone's body has its own 'time to go.' Ignoring the body's signals and refusing to accommodate its needs can lead to chronic constipation. The best time to pass stools is first thing in the morning, or 30 minutes after a meal. There are many treatments for constipation including medications. But the best approach is based on aiding the natural processes to push out the body waste.

Increasing the daily intake of fibre to at least 18-30g, drinking six to eight glasses of water a day, eating a diet rich in fibre and exercising daily should keep your digestive system on-the-go.

The world is moving faster, business is more demanding, and time is money — but don't put off a trip to the bathroom when you need to go.

Handwashing: The Why and the How

With today's high-tech approach to health care, it's easy to forget the simplest way to avoid infection — handwashing. With a little soap and water, you often can prevent what may take lots of time and money to cure.

Germs accumulate on your hands as you perform daily activities. By not washing hands, you can acquire or pass on a host of ailments, from the common cold to more serious such as an intestinal infection (dysentery) or inflammation of the liver (hepatitis).

Most cases of diarrhoea and vomiting are caused by inadequate handwashing.

Overall, infections claim more lives than any other disease except heart disease and cancer. Billions are spent annually to fight infections. More important than the monetary figure are the pain and suffering that often could be prevented by a minor expense on soap.

What's Proper Handwashing?
Thorough handwashing isn't simple. You must apply soap or detergent to your hands and rub vigorously for at least 10-20 seconds to suspend the germs (microorganisms). Then rinse them away. Follow the steps shown on the facing page for effective handwashing.

Germs tend to accumulate around cuticles, beneath fingernails and in the creases of your hands, so concentrate on these areas. Rinse all soap from your hands to remove as many microorganism as possible.

Water at about 110° F is the best to cut through the grease. Water hot enough to kill germs can actually harm your hands.

When Should You Wash?
It's impossible to keep your hands germ-free, but there are times when it's critical to wash your hands.

Always wash:

- Before you handle or eat food.
- After you visit the bathroom or change a diaper.
- After playing with a pet.
- After handling garbage.
- After handling money.
- After blowing your nose, sneezing or coughing into your hand.
- After handling uncooked food (especially meat).

Infections acquired in the hospital are very common. The Centers for Disease Control and Prevention of USA reports that annual direct costs of these infections average $4-5 to billion.

Remember, a little soap-and-water handwash can go a long way in keeping you healthy and disease free!

See also: DIARRHOEA: NATURE IS THE ANSWER; WHEN STOMACH DISAGREES; UNDERSTANDING FOOD POISONING.

7-steps for healthy, infection-free handwashing

1

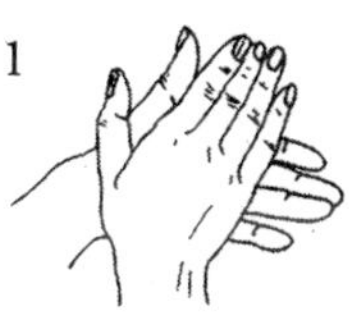

Rub palm to palm

2

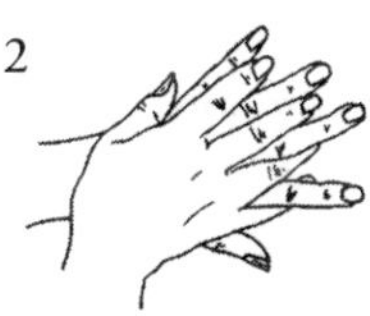

Rub the back of both palms

3

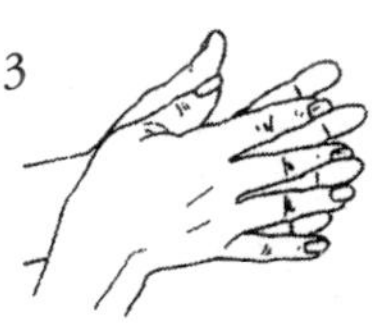

Rub palms again, fingers interlaced

4

Rub backs of inerlaced fingers

5

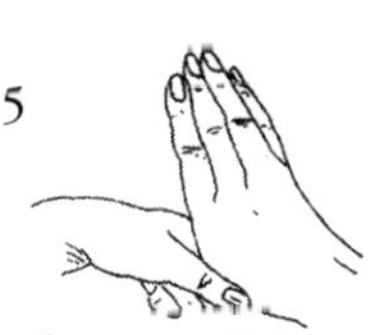

Remember to wash back thumbs

6

Rub both palms with fingertips

7. *Wash hands under running water using soap, rinse and dry throughly.*

Stop Bellyaching

The world is full of bellyaches and bellyaching, but there are some abdominal pains you shouldn't ignore. They can be symptoms of appendicitis or other potentially life-threatening conditions.

Sharp stomach pains that worsen when you move or wake you from a sound sleep could signal a dangerous problem — appendicitis or even a gall bladder or colon crisis, says Dr Lawrence R. Schiller, MD, of Baylor University Medical Centre, USA. If the pains are accompanied by fever, swelling, or tenderness; vomiting, diarrhoea, or a yellowing of your urine; or the whites of your eyes, contact your doctor immediately.

Do the same if you have sudden abdominal pain that radiates to your back or groin, especially if you feel light-headed.

Some of the suggestions given here may help prevent some types of abdominal pain: avoiding fatty or greasy foods; drinking plenty of water each day; eating small but more frequent meals; exercising regularly; limiting foods that produce gas; making sure that your meals are well-balanced and high in fibre or eating plenty of fruits and vegetables.

See also: WHEN STOMACH DISAGREES; DISCOURAGE GALLSTONES; HOW MANY KINDS OF PAIN ARE THERE.

A Moist Mouth Protects Against Cavities

What works 24/7 at fighting tooth decay? Saliva.

This oral fluid is rich in the minerals, calcium and phosphorus that reminerlise our pearly whites, and it neutralises acids produced by bacteria and sugars. But it is easily depleted when we become dehydrated from sports, medications, vomiting and stomach reflux. Here's how to treat a dry mouth:

Sip plain water often. Water keeps the mouth moist and loosens mucus.

Eat chewy or crunchy foods, like sugar-free gum, hard cheeses and raw vegetables to stimulate saliva flow.

Talk to your doctor or dentist about using a saliva substitute or topical gel for your gums. Some toothpastes, help maintain good levels of moisture in the mouth.

Don't smoke, drink too much alcohol or caffeinated drinks, or eat spicy foods. They only serve to dry out your mouth further.

Don't breathe through your mouth, if you can avoid it. It causes moisture in the mouth to dry out faster.

See also: TOOTH DECAY AND TOOTH ACHES; USE A GOOD TOOTHBRUSH AND USE IT WELL.

Woman's Crowning Glory

Hair, like the skin, owes its colour to melanin, the pigment that is formed in special cells. When the pigment cells become inactive, the hair turns white. This can happen due to ageing or reasons like illness, sudden shock or some internal disorder.

Hair has certain characteristics which we need to know. For one thing, hair is porous. This allows dyes and other lotions to penetrate the outer layer, causing the hair to be bleached, tinted or dyed but the many chemical ingredients in these products can damage both the texture and the look of the hair, making them dry, rough, brittle and lustreless. Hair also has elasticity. Styles and procedures which cause it to be stretched and pulled can damage it.

Hair is fed by the blood flowing to the follicle. That is why diet and a good blood circulation are so important. External care that we give helps to keep the scalp and hair in good condition. Thus, both internal and external health care are essential. Fatigue; stress and internal ill health are all reflected by the hair, as tension in the follicle muscles is affected.

This is what the 'world famous authority on beauty', Shahnaz Husain, writes in her international bestseller — *The Beauty Book:*

'Hair may be dry or greasy, according to the activity of the oil producing glands. Under-activity of the oil glands causes hair to dry, while over-activity makes it greasy, attracting dirt and causing other problems.

Dry hair, need plenty of nourishment. The roots, require extra oil and feeding. So, if you have dry hair, make it a point to use shampoos and tonics that have nutritive value, preferably with lanolin or vaseline bases. Egg shampoos go a long way towards preventing hair dryness.

Hot oil treatment, like massages with warm olive oil are extremely beneficial for toning dry hair and for preventing it from becoming brittle. It is a good idea to steam the scalp before a hot oil massage by placing the head in front of the basin of steaming hot water, or soaking a towel in steaming water and then wrapping it around the scalp. This is an excellent method for opening up the pores of the scalp.

On extremely dry hair, rub a little oil right into the roots before steaming. This encourages better and deeper absorption. Since it is a simple treatment it can be easily done at home.

Oily hair requires a completely different treatment. Though brushing is very good for healthy hair, too much brushing is not good for oily hair because it stimulates oil glands that are already over-active. So, go easy on the brush. Get yourself a good tonic especially blended for your type of hair. You must take care to buy something that will brace the scalp and prevent oiliness.

Oily hair needs to be washed every third or fourth day or even more frequently, depending on your individual comfort. A good, nourishing liquid shampoo is often the best answer.

Excessive oiliness, when neglected, often leads to falling hair and premature baldness, especially in men, after 35. Treated in time, loss can be checked considerably, though, lost hair cannot be replaced.'

Healthy, luxuriant hair is not difficult to achieve. Like all beauty assets, it needs constant care, and basic knowledge of its characteristics. Hair is like a beautiful, delicate fabric. Handle it that way.

The Harmful Effects of the Wrong Type of Protein

The mistake we make often is to get far too much of our protein from animal sources such as meat and milk. Not only is vegetable protein of a higher quality than animal protein, but good health can be maintained on a smaller amount of it. This reduces cost, wastes less energy in digestion, and creates fewer toxins.

Besides being superior to animal protein such as meats, eggs and milk, vegetable protein from lentils, nuts and vegetables is far easier to digest. Many vegetable protein sources, such as nuts and salads, can be eaten raw. Raw food typically has higher protein and other nutrients than cooked food.

Research has shown that a diet high in animal protein causes premature ageing. This is because animal proteins, especially meat, tend to produce toxins and acidity in the tissues, cause intestinal putrefaction and degeneration of the vital organs.

One of the best non-animal protein foods is soya milk. It is a high-protein food which is very nutritious, and has a low fat and high fibre content. It contains more protein than prime beef. Soya milk can be used on your cereal, for milk shakes and whenever milk is required in a recipe.

Raw nuts are another nutritious source of protein with twice the protein content of meat. They mix well with raisins or sultanas and are ideal as an energy snack.

With the protein power from legumes like beans, peas, lentils and whole pulses comes the added benefit of extra shot of fibre required by an adult. So, choose the healthier option — the vegetable protein.

See also: EAT YOUR COLOURS; LOVEABLE LEGUMES; MAGIC OF SPROUTS.

The Most Embarrassing Itch

An itchy groin can be most annoying and embarrassing for men of all ages. It often comes about in hot weather.

This itching is generally most intense in the crease of the skin between the leg and the genital area. This condition may develop due to the excessive sweating that one experiences in the groin region.

Generally, groin itch is caused by fungal infection and affects only the surface of the skin.

Using a medicated anti-fungal soap while bathing helps eliminate any germs present on the skin. Also make sure to dry the groin area well after a bath and dust it with anti-fungal powder. This will ensure that the area remains moisture free. Avoid using perfumed powders as the chemicals in these products aggravate the condition.

Don't scratch the rash as it will only make it worse.

Always wear loose-fitting, cotton undergarments and clothing that allow the skin to breathe. Avoid tight pants and other restrictive clothing.

Fungi loves sugar. The groin itch maybe relieved by cutting out refined carbohydrates and foods with high sugar content. It would also benefit to avoid alcohol since it converts into sugar in the body.

This itch usually responds promptly to these measures, but consulting a doctor is advised if it persists for more than two weeks.

See also: SWEATING AND BODY ODOUR.

Learn Doctor and Hospital Lingo

Have you ever been in the hospital when a doctor or nurse came in to discuss your ills — and you couldn't understand half of their words? Every profession has its own 'jargon,' and medicine is no exception.

Here are some common medical terms and their definitions.

iatrogenic: doctor-caused
Nosocomial: hospital-caused
NPO: patient receives no food or drink
h.s.: medication before sleep/at bedtime
i.v.: intravenous
i.m.: intramuscular
CVD: cardiovascular disease
T2DM: type 2 diabetes mellitus
BP: blood pressure
amp.: ampule
a.c.: before meals
b.c.: after meals
IC: inbetween meals
s.o.s.: whenever needed
p.r.n.: as needed/required
Medication schedule:

qid: four times daily;

tid: three times daily,

bid: twice daily;

od or *qd:* once daily;

qod: every other day;

stat: immediately

Whenever you, a family member or a loved one is in a hospital and you don't understand what a member of the medical staff has told you, ask her to explain it in a way that makes sense to you. It's her job.

See also: FIND THE BEST DOCTOR; TELL YOUR DOCTOR ALL THE FACTS.

Travel with a Medicine Kit

Take a well-stocked medicine kit with you when you travel.

A medicine kit can not only help keep you comfortable should you come down with a minor illness on your trip. It may even save your life.

You should use a waterproof container, preferably made of clear plastic, to help you find things more easily. If you take medication regularly, keep the amount you expect to use in the medicine kit and at least an equal amount in another bag — just in case you lose the kit. Also, ask your doctor for extra prescriptions.

Your medicine travel kit should include over-the-counter painkiller (such as aspirin, ibuprofen and acetaminophen), antacids, antibiotics, antihistamines, antiseptics, bandages, adhesive tape, gauze, decongestants, antidiarrhoeal medicines, feminine hygiene products, motion sickness pills, tweezers, a pocket knife and a thermometer.

A travel medicine kit is useful only if it is readily available when needed; it should be carried all the time while travelling.

See also: CLEAN OUT YOUR MEDICINE CABINET; HOME MEDICAL SUPPLIES.

Find the Best Doctor

Finding a good doctor is vital to your well-being. Yet many people put more effort into buying a car!

Unless you need a specialist for a chronic problem such as allergies, a general practitioner or a family physician is the best choice. That's because these doctors will have a broad spectrum of knowledge about a lot of different diseases and conditions. A 'generalist' will frequently cost less than a specialist, as well!

First, get recommendations from family, friends and neighbours. Second, make an appointment for an initial consultation. Third, take a list of important questions with you. And fourth, find out, if the physician is board-certified in a speciality, what hospitals the doctor is affiliated with and to which specialists and specialized medical centres patients are referred.

And don't be afraid to discuss money. You should know the doctor's fees and what insurance coverage will be accepted.

But above all, trust your instincts. Is this someone you trust and feel comfortable with? Are patients kept waiting a long time? Does the doctor spend adequate time with them? The answers to these questions are not measures of the doctor's politeness. They're indicators of attitude toward patients. A doctor who consistently overbooks patients so that people always have to wait — or, worse, never get enough time with the doctor to get their questions answered — is someone who may be more interested in the bottom line than in your health.

See also: TELL YOUR DOCTOR ALL THE FACTS; THE IMPORTANCE OF BEING CANDID.

Take it Easy

If you are impatient, competitive and hard on yourself (and maybe on others as well), it probably isn't easy for you to take it easy. But that doesn't mean you can't apply a little 'stopping power.'

How? Take a quiet break during the day. A quiet moment of meditation in the office will make you more productive during the workday. A peaceful period will help a homemaker stand up to the stress of managing a household and caring for children and a spouse. And a few minutes of quiet will prevent a vacation that is crammed with activities from becoming physically and emotionally draining instead of rejuvenating. People who are always on the go may soon burn out and be gone!

Medical research has shown that stress (your body's chemical response to certain life situations) can contribute to some forms of cardiovascular disease and make you 'coronary-prone.' Stressors — situations that trigger stress — raise blood pressure, heart rate, blood flow and metabolism rate. If stressors provoke these physiological changes too frequently and too strongly, many doctors believe they can lead to heart disease.

At Stanford University School of Medicine, patients were taught a simple relaxation technique that helped them significantly reduce their blood pressure. While they imagined a tranquil scene, they tensed and then relaxed their muscles. The patients practising this technique lowered their blood pressure twice as much as the patients who received medical treatment but no instruction in relaxation techniques.

If you find yourself reacting strongly to everyday events and having a hard time relaxing, talk to your doctor about some relaxation techniques you can learn to help you take it easy.

Spice Up Your Health with Cinnamon

Cinnamon *(dalchini)* has been used since ancient times in Indian, Greek, Italian and Moroccan cooking. This delectably aromatic spice is frequently used in baked foods, cereals and herbal teas.

Cinnamon has also long been known to have medicinal, benefits. It possesses carminative, antiulcer and antivomitive properties. It increases circulation, reduces flatulence, acidity, helps control diarrhoea and may even reduce pain from menstrual cramps. Cinnamon also serves as a good mouth freshner.

The oil of cinnamon is responsible for stimulating saliva and gastric juices which facilitates digestion. In addition, cinnamon oil has shown evidence of antibacterial action. It can help fight staphylococcal germs and *Candida albicans,* or thrush. Some people claim that cinnamon even acts as an aphrodisiac. Cinnamon oil, warm water and honey is beneficial in cold.

'Recent research suggests that cinnamon maybe helpful as a supplement to regular diabetes treatment in people with type-2 diabetes,' says Dr. Maria Collazo-Clavell, an endocrinologist with Mayo Clinic, USA.

Add the spice of cinnamon to your diet, and add to your health and joy in life.

See also: THE DOCTOR IN YOUR KITCHEN; PUT PEEPER ON YOUR PAIN; WHAT HONEY CAN DO FOR YOU.

Put Pepper on Your Pain

In the 1600s, Montezuma put hot chili peppers in his hot chocolate. In the 1800s, Irish doctors use them for tooth pain. And today, American doctors use capsaicin — the active painkilling ingredient in peppers — to relieve pain from rheumatoid arthritis, osteoarthritis and shingles.

Researchers think that capsaicin blocks pain by depleting one of the chemicals your body needs to send pain signals to the brain. In one study of 100 patients with arthritis who used *Zostrix,* (limited availability in India) a drug that contains capsaicin, 57 per cent of the participants experienced reduced pain. They were able to perform daily tasks more easily, and some were even able to exercise regularly after using capsaicin.

A number of over-the-counter products contain capsaicin as the active ingredient. Ask your doctor or your pharmacist to help you choose one.

See also: KNOW WHAT PAIN KILLERS TO TAKE; HOW MANY KINDS OF PAIN ARE THERE.

Pray or Meditate

Maybe science isn't really opposite to faith, after all. New research in medical science supports the ancient belief that there is a role for prayer and meditation in healing.

Studies indicate, for example, that seriously ill people are more likely to get well if they're prayed for than if they're not — even if they don't know that anyone is praying for them!

In fact, prayer is apparently such a powerful tool that some doctors even incorporate prayer into treatment plans for their patients.

No matter what your religious affiliation, or whether you are religious at all, you may find the act of praying comforting and relaxing, and it may even be a good way to relieve chronic pain. A wide range of books and materials is available to get you started. Pick up either of these books at a bookstore or library and explore the possibility of prayer or meditation in your life.

The Raw Food Diet

Benefits from raw food diet are based on the premise that the healthiest form of food is uncooked. Cooking is thought to destroy or limit the enzymes naturally present in the food.

Raw food prevents and cures disease by virtue of its enzyme content, its wide variety and abundance of nutrients, its low fat and sugar content and its ability to eliminate toxins.

Recent studies have shown that a diet high in raw food is effective in the treatment of sugar metabolic disease such as hypoglycaemia and borderline diabetes, as well as for ulcers, obesity and even cancer — especially if the diet is high in carrot juice and foods containing chlorophyll, such as sprouts and wheat germ.

Raw food diet includes beans, dried fruits, fresh fruit and vegetables, fresh juices, grams, legumes, coconut, milk, nuts, seeds, sun-ripen foods and other natural food which has not been processed.

Preparing diet of raw food is not difficult. Many of us do it regularly yet unknowingly. The food is prepared by soaking and sprouting, fermenting, pickling, juicing and chopping and blending it in the food processor into smoothies or soups.

Such diet is a potent remedy for chronic fatigue. In one study of patients with chronic fatigue, who were put on a diet high in raw food most reported a considerable increase in their energy levels.

Because of its rich supply of enzymes a diet rich in raw food helps slow down the ageing process. It is extremely nourishing, low in calories and causes more efficient fat metabolism; as the brain is better nourished, thinking becomes clearer and memory improves. And to top it all you tend to be slimmer — the safe natural way.

The Doctor in Your Kitchen

Who would have guessed that the favourite ingredient in Indian cuisine is also the world's most popular herbal panacea? The world production of garlic now exceeds 2 million tonnes.

For over 3000 years garlic has been a part of Ayurvedic tradition. It is mentioned in the Bible and in an Egyptian medical papyrus dating about 1500 B.C. which lists twenty-two different garlic preparations for ailments including heart disease, worms and tumours. Hakim Ibn Sina, father of Unnani Tibb wrote about its medicinal properties in the 11th century in his five volume *Cannon of Medicine*, one of the most famous medical books in human history.

The antiseptic properties of garlic were demonstrated during the Great Plague of Europe in the 17th century. It was observed that those who had stores of garlic in their cellars, by and large, survived.

During the two world wars garlic was taken by wounded soldiers with excellent results.

Modern research has validated this history of garlic and shown that it is effective for these conditions.

The future of garlic is also promising. According to more than a dozen recent studies, cholesterol levels are reduced by regular intake of garlic. Recently it's also been found that the AIDS virus does not grow well in the presence of garlic in tissue culture.

Garlic is an antibiotic. Allicin is its active medicinal component and much research has been done into its antibiotic, antifungal and anticancer effects. Newer discoveries have extended the list of garlic compounds to more than four hundred, with at least thirty of them with known medicinal properties. Most of garlic's medicinal constituents result from the breakdown of allicin.

Garlic reduces heart disease by lowering blood cholesterol levels and reducing blood-clotting tendencies. It has the ability to remove cholesterol from the walls of the arteries and thin the blood. At least five compounds of garlic have been shown to lower cholesterol synthesis in the liver, including allicin, ajoene and diallyl disulfide.

The sulphur compounds in garlic helps to fight cancer. The Greek physician Hippocrates recommended garlic for cancer more than 2000 years ago, but not until the 20th century could the scientists find reasons why it might be helpful. It has been shown to activate natural killer-cell activity against cancer cells, with an increase of upto 50 per cent against some tumour cells. It stimulates the immune system which has a rejuvenating effect on the body. It also helps to increase endurance.

Scientific studies in the last decade have supported the idea that garlic is a tonic — that it can reduce symptoms of stress, improve energy levels, reduce fatigue, improve athletic performance, and extend life expectancy.

How much and in what form should we take garlic? Even just one gram (about one clove) of garlic per day has a beneficial effect on health, although for a maximum effect, two cloves per day are recommended.

Raw garlic can be taken as a crushed clove mixed in your food, or as one 1000-mg tablet. To take cooked garlic, just cook the garlic with your food, or cook it on its own in a microwave oven for about half a minute.

The research into medicinal effects of garlic continues; but the bottom line is that whole is greater than its parts. The constituents work together with overlapping effects.

See also: SPICE UP YOUR HEALTH WITH CINNAMON; PUT PEPPER ON YOUR PAIN; WHAT HONEY CAN DO FOR YOU.

Do Some Heavy-Lifting Housework

Researchers at the Mayo Clinic in Minnesota, USA, have released the results of a recent study that shows that women who run, swim and perform aerobic exercises such as dancing have less back strength than homemakers. Homemakers who carry their babies and lift heavy loads day after day appear to be more fit than their aerobicizing sisters; you can be aerobically fit and yet not be strong.

The researchers' results show that the homemakers had more upper-body and arm strength usually associated with back strength from weight-bearing exercises. Bones lose calcium and weaken with age, but strength or weight bearing exercises can help slow and sometimes even reverse this trend. There are additional benefits. Not only do these exercises make a person look and feel better, but their performance in everyday activities such as climbing stairs and carrying weight also improves. The homemakers' heavy-lifting housework decreases their risk of developing osteoporosis.

Stronger muscles also mean better mobility and balance, thus a lower risk of falling and getting injured. More lean body mass aids in weight control because each kilo of muscle burns more calories than its equivalent weight in fat. So in addition to going to the gym or exercising at home, lift that laundry and tote those groceries with gusto!

See also: LIFTING PROPERLY.

Doing Nothing Can be Deadly

An inactive lifestyle is a prominent risk factor for cardiovascular disease. One study found inactivity to be a more important gauge of death than any other cardiovascular disease risk factor. The least fit men and women in the study were nearly twice as likely to die of cardiovascular disease as were their fit counterparts. Poor physical fitness was a greater cardiovascular risk factor than were high blood pressure, high cholesterol, obesity and family history.

Regular exercise is important in preventing heart disease. The American Heart Association recommends 30-60 minutes of aerobic exercise three to four times per week to promote cardiovascular fitness. Walking is a good start to break from the usual sedentary routine. For the first week, walk for 10 minutes in three to four days and increase to 15 minutes throughout the next week and so on.

Increased physical fitness was also shown to counter the negative effects of other cardiovascular risk factors. Moderately fit smokers with high cholesterol, for instance, lived longer than did healthy but inactive nonsmokers.

See also: AEROBIC VS ANAEROBIC EXERCISE; ADD YEARS TO YOUR LIFE AT LUNCHTIME; BE FLEXIBLE AND LIVE TO BE 100.

Use a Security Blanket

We all need comfort sometime during the day, and a 'solacing object' may bring you the security you need.

For a child, a 'security blanket' may be a blanket, a favourite toy or a book or a doll. For an adult, it may be a photograph of a spouse or children or a paperweight that sits on the desk as a reminder of a good friend.

All of these are examples of what are called solacing objects. And although they may seem sentimental, they are eminently practical because they can evoke powerful memories of happy times with loving family members and close friends. The emotions that are stirred by the memories can help relieve pain, reduce anxiety, fight depression and sometimes bring feelings of peacefulness and safety.

At times in this chaotic world, we each need to feel safe. Keep something with you that will bring you comfort when you most need it.

See also: CHERISH YOUR FRIENDS.

Stop Eating Before You're Full

The Japanese have a saying — *hara hachi bu*. It is a Confucian teaching that counsels people to stop eating when they are 80 per cent full. The Ayurvedic tradition advises eating until you are 75 per cent full; the Chinese specify 70 per cent; and Arab tradition describes a full belly as one that contained one-third food, one-third liquid, and one-third air — in other words, nothing.

Also, the French may have something to teach us. To say 'I'm hungry' you say *'J'ai faim'* — 'I have hunger' — and when you are finished you do not say that you are full, but *'Je n'ai plus faim'* — 'I have no more hunger.' That is a completely different way of thinking about satiety. So, ask yourself not, 'Am I full?' but, 'Is my hunger gone?' That moment will arrive several bites sooner.

The people of Okinawa (the indigenous people of Ryukyu islands in Japan) are the only ones who practice *hara hachi bu* for calorie restriction. Almost one third of Okinawans live to be one hundred; their heart disease rates are 80 per cent lower than the western societies; the rates of cancer are 50-80 per cent lower, specially breast, colon, ovarian and prostate cancer.

The traditional Okinawa diet with its emphasis on vegetables, whole grains, fruits, legumes and fish with limited lean meats is a model for healthy eating and healthy ageing.

Slow down when you eat. Listen to your body and give your brain time to signal that you are full. Take small bites of your food. Thoroughly chew your food and pay attention to the taste of each bite. If you are eating with family or friends, participate fully in the conversation rather than eating quickly. Do all your eating at a table and not in front of a television.

Aaachoo! Is It a

Both are viral, upper

	Cold
Usual symptoms	• Runny nose, sneezing, nasal congestion • Sore throat (usually scratchy) • Cough • No fever or low fever • Mild fatigue
Caused by	One of more than 200 viruses typically causes 2 to 4 colds a year in adults and 4 to 8 a year in kids
Seriousness	Usually not serious except in people with lung disease or other serious illness
Can I work?	Usually you can, but use care to avoid spreading a cold to others. Wash hands frequently
Is it preventable?	Possibly, through careful handwashing, not sharing food, towels or handkerchiefs and getting good nutrition and enough rest
Do antibiotics help?	No, not unless you also have a bacterial infection
Self-care	• Drink plenty of warm liquids. Homemade soup can help clear mucus. • Increase sleep and rest. • Use cold remedies cautiously.

When to Seek Medical Help?
If symptoms persist beyond 10 days or you experience difficulty in breathing, faintness, severe sore throat, cough producing a lot of sputum or mucus (especially if green or yellow), pain in the face or a chronic health condition, then seek medical help.

Cold or the Flu?

respiratory tract infections

Flu, Influenza

- Runny nose and sneezing
- Sore throat, cough and headache
- Fever (usually more than 101°F) and chills
- Moderate to severe fatigue and weakness
- Achy muscles

One of a few viruses from the influenza A or influenza B family. On average, adults have less than one infection a year

Can be serious. A special concern in elderly people and those with chronic health conditions

No, not until fever, fatigue and all but the mild symptoms have resolved

Usually, through vaccination.

Sometimes. Antiviral antibiotics are available, but work only if taken at the onset of the illness.

- Drink plenty of fluids to avoid dehydration.
- Increase sleep and rest.
- Use over-the-counter pain relievers cautiously, as needed.

Care against Pneumonia

Pneumonia can occur after a cold or flu or on its own. It can be caused by viruses, bacteria or other organisms. Typical symptoms are prominent cough with a lot of phlegm. Fever is common. If you are concerned about pneumonia, seek medical help.

Practice Kitchen Caution

Bacteria, viruses, moulds and yeast in food cause many cases of food poisoning. You can keep this from happening to you and your family by following these simple suggestions.

- Always use a fresh kitchen towel when cooking.
- Don't keep food at room temperature for more than sixty minutes — before or after cooking.
- Keep the marinated poultry and other meats in the refrigerator. Take out only before cooking.
- Don't reuse marinade without first bringing it to a boil.

Microwaves are convenient, but bacteria can grow in microwave-cooked foods because these devices cook foods unevenly. Although food cooks quickly, some parts of the food may not be cooked at all. Bacteria and other microorganisms in the uncooked portions can then cause food poisoning.

To prevent this from happening, always thaw frozen food before cooking them in the microwave. Cover the cooking vessel you use with a lid or with plastic wrap made for use in microwaves. This will trap steam and help cook the food properly. Leave the lid slightly ajar or poke a hole in the plastic wrap to allow ventilation. When you remove food from microwave, let it stand. The food will continue to cook for several minutes.

See also: PAY ATTENTION TO FLOOR SAFETY.

The Importance of Being Candid

Your doctor needs a complete picture of everything in your life that could conceivably affect your mental and physical functioning. Otherwise, recommended treatment for various problems that arise may be ineffective.

A survey at Harvard University revealed that most doctors think they spend more than ten minutes talking and listening to their patients during appointment. The researchers found that in reality, doctors spend less than two minutes.

Since your doctor may not be taking the time to get all the information he needs to help you, take the initiative. Tell your physician about the things you think are important.

For example, let your doctor know: If you live alone, eat a lot of junk food or feel stressed out. Tell him if and how much you exercise, drink or smoke. Talk about your feelings and emotional life. Is your sex life satisfying? Are you worried about your kids? Tell him about your job and professional pressures if any.

Similarly surgery is always serious and risky. Among the questions you should ask the surgeon are: What risks do you face? What kinds of complications can occur? Do some of the patients choose not to have the suggested procedure? And why? What other options are available? How long before you get back to normal?

Taking a second opinion is always a good idea. Do not feel diffident about it. Doctors are now described as 'health care providers' and patients as 'consumers.' Medicine is more of a business now than ever. Protect yourself by asking questions.

See also: FIND THE BEST DOCTOR; LEARN DOCTOR AND HOSPITAL LINGO.

Sleep Like a Baby

If you are having trouble sleeping, you may have tried over-the-counter sleeping aids or drugs to help you sleep, but they haven't worked. You may even have tried herbal remedies, meditation and relaxation exercises but still find yourself lying in bed at night staring at the ceiling, unable to sleep. You wish you could just sleep like a baby — and that may be the precise answer to your problem!

You may be sleeping in the wrong position. A fitness expert at the Massachusetts Institute of Technology suggests that you sleep in the fetal position. Instead of lying on your back or stomach, go to sleep on your side, knees bent at right angles to your body.

If you still continue to have trouble sleeping, here are five surefire strategies to knock you out.

First, learn to associate your bed with rest, quiet and sleep. Don't eat in bed or take work to bed.

Second, make your bedroom comfortable and conducive to sleep. Keep the temperature at around 68° F and make sure your mattress is comfortable.

Third, stick to a regular sleep schedule. During the work week and on weekends, go to sleep at the same time and wake up at the same time.

Fourth, if you can't fall asleep soon after going to bed, get up and leave the bedroom. Read or watch a little TV, but don't do it in your bedroom.

Fifth, avoid alcohol, caffeine, tea and cola drinks and exercise late in the day. They all interfere with sleep.

If you follow these tips, occasional insomnia should trouble you no more. But see a doctor if insomnia persists.

Never Mix Aspirin and Vitamin C

Aspirin has been around for over one hundred years and is widely accepted as a useful drug for treating pain. People around the world are routinely prescribed low-dose aspirin to prevent heart attack or strokes.

During the cold and flu season, you get lots of advice on how to fight the symptoms that come with these illnesses. Many people swear by vitamin C for both prevention and treatment, and most people will take an aspirin or two at some point during a bout with any illness.

But both vitamin C and aspirin are acids. Vitamin C is ascorbic acid, and aspirin is acetylsalicylic acid. And if you take these two substances at the same time, they can irritate your stomach. Researchers have found that heavy doses — which people often take to fight cold and flu symptoms — can produce severe stomach irritation that may lead to the development of ulcers.

Care is advised before taking aspirin and vitamin C together.

See also: DON'T GIVE ASPIRIN TO A CHILD WITH A FEVER; HOW DOES ASPIRIN BENEFIT THE HEART; THE MULTI-TALENTED VITAMIN C.

Make a Healthy Soup

Soup not only tastes 'mmm-mmm-good,' it can keep you healthy, too. Soups are a good source of minerals and vitamins.

Vegetable soup is packed with almost every vitamin that you need. The vegetables, beans and rice in some soups give you the fibre you need in your diet.

If you add a little bit of chicken to a vegetable soup or vegetables to a chicken soup, you enhance the health-promoting qualities of soup even more. The protein in chicken, along with the carbohydrates and fibre in vegetables, makes homemade soup almost a perfect meal. In addition, some studies show that having a bowl of soup before a main course can even help you lose weight.

Soup can help you slow down. Having a bowl of soup involves spooning, slurping, smelling, tasting, chewing, and swallowing. This helps you slow down your eating time. Slower eaters tend to notice signs of fullness sooner and consume fewer calories by better enjoying their food in the moment.

Soups stimulate the senses. These warm concoctions have unique aromas, tastes, enjoyable temperatures and visual interest, which add to the pleasure you experience when eating.

There's something reassuring about a bowl of hot soup, no matter how you slurp it.

See also: HAVE A HEALTHY SNACK; BE A HEALTHY SHOPPER.

Look Good for Fun and Profit

Take time every morning to make sure that you look your best. Researchers have discovered that how you look can affect your inner chemistry. Wear something that makes you feel comfortable and makes you feel happy to look in the mirror. Show people that you care about your appearance. When you feel good about yourself, your body produces more of its own natural 'feel good' chemicals — endorphins — which make you feel confident and relaxed.

Researchers have found that paying attention to how you look can pay off in cash as well. According to researchers at Michigan State University, people who look good earn more money than those who do not. This advantage includes not only models and actors but also office and factory workers, engineers and even telemarketers.

Sociologists have noted that people make assessments within a short time of encountering you — measured in seconds. Once that opinion has been formed it is very difficult to shake off — evidence tends to be interpreted in line with the initial assessment. They have also found that in terms of initial reaction, looks *do* matter. The better you look, the more likely you are to form lasting relationships or even find a partner.

Even as we grow older and realize looks aren't everything, it certainly doesn't hurt to have an image that's easy on the eyes. Fortunately, being good-looking these days isn't just about being born that way. It's about appreciating and emphasizing your best features, and putting your best foot forward.

See also: FOREVER YOUNG; LIVE WITH NATURE.

Avoid 'Guaranteed' Weight Loss Plans

Are you considering a diet plan that 'absolutely guarantees' that you'll lose weight quickly and easily?

Are you tempted to start a weight loss plan that is based on a new miracle food or drink that will help you lose a lot of weight in a short period of time? If you answered yes to either question, please think again.

Why? Because the diet won't work. Decades of research at centres all across the world has shown that there are two key factors in any successful weight loss plan:

1. You need to evaluate your eating habits and make permanent changes, and
2. You need to develop a program of regular moderate aerobic exercise that works for you.

Any other approach generally means you'll lose weight initially, then gain back more than you lost.

There are two other important facts to be kept in mind. People over the age of forty can weigh upto five kilos more than they did in their twenties and still be in good shape. In fact, because fat contributes to higher estrogen levels, a woman who weighs a bit more may experience fewer menopausal symptoms and have a lower risk of developing osteoporosis than if she weighed less.

Although the media glamorizes thinness, you may be better off carrying a few extra kilos. Ask your doctor to help you figure out your optimum weight.

See also: LOSE WEIGHT GRADUALLY; UNEXPECTED WEIGHT CHANGES.

Slash the Fat

You can hardly read about nutrition, diet or cooking without being reminded of the importance of reducing fat in your diet. But for some people, a meal is not really a meal unless it includes meat. And the salad must be dressed with delicious tasting dressing without realising that many dressings are high in fat.

What can you do?

Nutritional experts generally agree that your total fat intake should not come to more than 30 per cent of your total daily calories. You can still eat meat regularly — a couple of times a week — and meet the nutritional recommendations concerning dietary fat if you trim all obvious fat; choose only lean cuts; bake or broil meat instead of frying and keep portions small.

The majority of salad dressings available in the market contain high levels of fat. In fact, some dressings get as much as 90 per cent of their calories from fat nearly three times the amount they should! You can avoid that problem by making your own healthy low-fat salad dressings.

There are many different recipes for healthy salad dressings. For a healthy creamy dressing, substitute plain nonfat yogurt for fattier dairy products, then spice it up with a mixture of onion, dill, garlic, basil, oregano and pepper.

See also: FATS: THE GOOD AND THE BAD; THE RAW FOOD DIET; ADOPT AN ESKIMO DIET.

Chronic Fatigue: Begin a New Innings

Never start your day under time pressure. Start your day early.

Always reserve a few minutes for traffic hold-ups, time delays on other people's part and if still need be, reschedule your day's plan. A rush schedule saps a lot of energy, and quite unnecessarily.

Set clear goals for each day. Take time each morning to set specific goals for the day. Determine what you want to do; do not let the routine control you. You may have to change this now and then, but just grin and accept it, never letting it go too far. Remember, you can never please everybody, but the bottom line is: Your employer is the boss, he pays for your time.

Tackle one thing at a time. Many a time you feel fatigued just because you think, 'I have so much to do, where should I start and how will I ever complete it.' The remedy is simple. Make a list, set your priorities and chart your progress, giving your best to the job at hand. Before long all your tasks will be done and you would still feel energetic.

Drink Up

Is your workplace hot — at least in terms of temperature? If it is, you should drink lots of water, especially if you're a man.

Two-thirds of our planet and two-thirds of your body are composed of water. It is probably the most essential of all the essential nutrients.

Your body needs water for proper digestion, to keep mucous membranes moist, to dispose off bodily wastes and to perspire, a process that keeps your body cool. Water is also essential for a healthy bloodstream.

Dehydration occurs when water intake is less than water loss. Symptoms of dehydration include dry lips and tongue; headache; weakness, dizziness, or extreme fatigue; concentrated urine that appears darker than normal; nausea and muscle cramps.

Drink plenty of water to hydrate your body. Or you can opt for natural drinks like buttermilk, coconut water, fruit juice or lime water. Electrolyte solutions and ORS (salt and sugar solutions) are good options to replace lost minerals.

Consume fruits and vegetables rich in water content, such as watermelons, oranges and cucumbers. Avoid beverages containing caffeine or alcohol, especially in the summer.

Finally try and inculcate the good habit of drinking at least eight glasses of water every day, specially if you perspire a lot and in the summer season.

Tailor Your Chair, Tailor Your Desk

You can prevent or minimize back, neck and leg pain by ensuring that you always sit in a chair that gives your back the support it needs and by making sure your desk at home and on the job is at the right height.

The best kind of chair to use is a firm recliner that has a contoured support and adjustable lower back cushion.

The best way to tell if your desk is appropriate for you is to check:

When seated at your desk, your feet should be able to rest comfortably on the floor. Your desk should be 7-12 inches or 17-30 cm above the seat of your chair. If you work at a keyboard, it should be at elbow level when you're sitting. And you should not have to lean forward to work at your desk. This will put unnecessary strain on your neck and back. Instead, try to keep your shoulders relaxed and your head in line with your spine.

If you do a lot of sitting in your car — commuting to and from work or shuttling the kids or ageing parents around the neighbourhood — check out the design of your seat. You need a seat that gives support to the curve of your spine.

Almost all manufacturers now pay attention to designing car seats. But the best way to find what suits you is to pay attention to seat design when you are test-driving a car.

Paying attention to these little details can pay off by preventing a great deal of pain and discomfort.

See also: MINIMIZING EARLY MORNING BACKACHE.

5 Secrets of Optimising Nutrition

Here are five simple facts on nutrition to achieve optimum nutrition without having to sacrifice the enjoyment of food.

Eat slowly. This leads to a more thorough breakdown of the food, resulting in release of more nutrients and hence better nourishment.

Have a balanced diet. About 50 per cent of the diet should consist of fruit since it is nourishing, easily digested and produces no toxins in the body. Vegetables and whole grains should comprise about 20 per cent each, and high protein foods about 10 per cent. Fat will take care of itself, since all foods contain some fat and we need very little.

Limit fat and sugar intake. Excess fat causes reduced blood flow to all parts of the body, resulting in disease and premature ageing. Excess sugar results in fatigue and sugar metabolic diseases and is converted to fat by the body, causing even more problems.

Emphasise raw food. Raw food such as fruit, salad, bean sprouts and raw nuts should make up about 70 per cent of your total diet. Raw foods have no nutrient loss from processing and heating.

Get the most from your fresh food. To keep valuable nutrients at peak levels in produce, pick vegetables that are crisp and firm and avoid soft, bruised food. And since fruits and vegetables spoil quickly if left at room temperature, keep them refrigerated. If you have limited storage in your refrigerator, make it a habit to stop by the market every day or two. Better long term health will make it worth the effort.

By following these recommendations your health and vitality will improve and you will look younger.

Grandma Knows Best

Reach for tea and honey! Every grandmother knows this remedy. Any warm beverage can make a sore throat feel better, but tea is especially good because it contains compounds called tannins, which can ease the irritation. Add honey to tea to coat your throat with a soft, soothing, protective layer.

If you want to go caffeine free or prefer herbal treatment, try any of the following from the vast repertoire of natural remedies for soothing relief.

Liquorice *(mulethi)* is a recognized home remedy for sore throat in the Indian sub-continent and many other Asian cultures. A small piece of raw liquorice is chewed or sucked for treating this condition. The healing property of the herb soothes inflammation quickly.

The leaves of holy basil *(tulsi)* have been found to be beneficial for soothing sore throat. Water boiled with basil leaves taken as a drink, and used as a gargle will relieve a sore throat.

A gargle prepared from fenugreek seeds *(methi dana)* is a very effective remedy for treating a sore throat. To prepare this gargle, simmer two tablespoons of fenugreek seeds in a litre of cold water for half an hour on a low flame. This should then be allowed to cool to a bearable temperature, strained, and then used entirely as a gargle.

See also: WHAT HONEY CAN DO FOR YOU; PROTECT YOUR VOCAL CHORDS; SPICE UP YOUR LIFE WITH CINNAMON.

Feast on Fibre

Almost everyone these days is trying to increase the amount of fibre they eat. Officially, fibre is a type of carbohydrate that body cannot digest. According to Harvard School of Public Health most adult women should aim for 20 grams of fibre a day; men for over 30 grams. When you eat a balanced, healthy diet, you usually get most fibre you need, which also means you will be losing your risk of diabetes, heart disease and constipation. Not bad at all.

If you find it difficult to get enough fibre, try these six easy ways to get what you need.

One, get whole grains for breakfast cereals. Or if you can't do that, try corn, brown rice or whole-wheat pasta at lunch or dinner. Whole legumes, *dals* and beans, sprouts are rich with fibre.

Two, eat the whole fruit instead of drinking fruit juices. Whole apples and whole oranges are packed with lot more fibre and lot fewer calories then their liquid form. Strawberries, raspberries, blackberries, plums, papaya, melon and guava can also enhance fibre intake.

Three, eat vegetables that have edible stems, such as cauliflower, broccoli, and lotus stem.

Four, when possible, eat the skins of potatoes and other vegetables.

Five, always eat whole-wheat and other whole-grain breads.

Six, eat more beans. It's easy to forget about beans, but they are a great tasting cheap source not only of fibre but good carbohydrates, protien and other important nutrients.

Follow these six easy pieces of advice, and you'll get the fibre you need.

Have a Healthy Snack

Some nutritionists counsel against having snacks during the day because most available snack foods are not nutritious and some are even unhealthy for you. But others argue that eating more frequently during the day may actually be better for you.

If you want to snack, keep in mind that all snacks don't have to consist of fattening foods.

You can have an apple or an orange instead of your favourite fast food. Or you can eat popcorn instead of potato chips. And a slice of vegetarian pizza can be just as tasty as sausage pizza, but it's better for you.

Another healthier option when you have the 'hungries' is to treat yourself to a belly-filling potato instead of a pile of potato chips. Potatoes are extremely nutritious and low in fat, and one potato has only 200 calories! Research has shown that potatoes are also rich in vitamin B, potassium and iron. They are also fair sources of fibre and protein and provide half of your daily requirement of vitamin C.

So the next time you're in the mood for a snack, grab a potato, wash it, pierce its skin with a fork and pop it into the microwave. In less than ten minutes, you'll have a healthy treat.

Then top it with a full-flavoured salsa or smooth nonfat yogurt. You'll be surprised at how delicious it tastes!

If it helps you feel better during the day, go ahead and snack. But make sure your snacks are nutritious as well as delicious.

See also: BE A HEALTHY SHOPPER; MAKE A HEALTHY SOUP.

Earwax: Digging Out is not the Answer

Earwax (medically referred to as cerumen) is a naturally produced substance that helps filter dust, sweat, shampoo etc. and protects the ear canal from infection. Normally earwax is self-draining and drains by itself. Children tend to produce a lot of earwax which tapers off as they grow older; it is softer and higher than the earwax produced by adults.

Earwax can be a serious problem if too much is produced; it may impede the passage of sound in the ear canal. If you can actually see wax in the outer part of the ear, or if your hearing seems to be getting worse or you hear ringing or other noises, you need to see your doctor.

Excess earwax is best removed by softening it up. Excess earwax can get nearly rock-hard, making it difficult to remove. To soften the wax, a few drops of mineral oil, baby oil, or glycerin are put in the ear with an eyedropper, the head rolled around to let the oil soak in. Doing this twice a day for several days, will make the wax much softer and it will start moving toward the outside of the ear, where it's easier to remove.

Blockage of earwax occurs when the wax gets pushed deep within the ear canal. The most common cause of this is the use of foreign objects in the ear canal (bobby pins, rolled napkin corners) which pushes the wax deeper in the ear canal. Earwax blockage affects about 6 per cent of people and is the most common ear problem doctors see.

Hearing aid and earplug users are also more prone to earwax blockage.

The doctor may remove earwax with a small plastic spoon called curette, or by irrigating the ear with warm water, saline, sodium bicarbonate or prescription eardrops.

Get Up and Get Going

Exercise is a great way to start your day. But if it is true (which it is) that the 300 calories you burn exercising in the evening, are the same as working them off in the morning, then what is the big deal about making exercise routine a morning activity?

Experts say that there are real physical and psychological benefits of morning exercise. By exercising in the morning you jump-start your metabolism and it can stay on the upswing for the rest of the day. With a metabolism on the move, you burn more calories through the day, even when you're off the treadmill.

Researchers at an Arizona Health Institute conducted a study that revealed that people who exercised in the morning were more likely to stick with their daily workouts than people who worked out later.

Morning exercisers also report that it helps them to keep their appetite on an even keel — they tend to snack, even binge, less. Not only do they eat less (since activity causes the release of endorphins, which in turn diminishes appetite), they also choose healthier portions of healthier foods.

Studies have shown that exercise significantly increases mental sharpness. Exercising in the morning means you start your day without mental fogginess.

If you have a hard time getting motivated in the morning, lay out your workout clothes next to your bed the night before, so they are the first things you see when you wake up in the morning. Once you discover the benefits of exercising in the morning, you'll look forward to your morning workout.

See also: AEROBIC VS ANAEROBIC EXERCISE; TRY AN ANTI-AGEING 'PILL'.

Don't Be So Sweet

Concentrated sugar can be described as empty calories which have a drug-like effect on the body. And our body is not set up to handle concentrated sugars.

Although 'sugar' (not refined) is the fuel that runs our entire body, using concentrated sugar overloads the delicate mechanism and the pancreas overreacts by producing too much insulin.

On an average we eat a lot of sugar — much of it unconsciously. That's because about 75 per cent of the sugar we eat is added to foods before we ever see it: ketchup, soups, salad dressings, canned and frozen fruits and vegetables, juices and many other food items contain sugar.

Fruit juices may seem like nutritious sources of vitamins and minerals, but they are super-concentrated in naturally occurring sugar — making them less healthy than you'd think.

Nutritionists disagree on sugar in the diet. Some believe sugar is okay if you have a healthy diet, while others think it contributes to cavities and diseases such as obesity, diabetes, high blood cholesterol and hypertension.

While the debate goes on, you can substitute fresh fruits for sugary snacks and get carbohydrates from healthy foods instead of 'empty calories' from sugar. Replace sugar with the sweet alternatives like honey on cereals and in drinks. Reduce your intake of foods with a high sugar content such as sweets, cakes, soft drinks and alcohol.

See also: LEARN WARNING SIGNS OF DIABETES; EAT FOODS THAT WILL EVENTUALLY ROT.

Stay Calm and Live Longer

Do you explode every time the slightest thing goes wrong? Do you have a cynical attitude toward people?

If you have answered yes to either of these questions, you may have to change your way of thinking and behaving if you want to live a long and satisfying life.

Angry, cynical people are five times as likely to die before age fifty as people who are calm and trusting, according to studies undertaken by a psychiatrist at the Duke University Medical Center. The studies indicate that acting out anger toward others and a cynical mistrust of people are strong predictors of premature death.

According to a study published in American Heart Associated's journal, fiery-tempered individuals are more likely to suffer a cardiac arrest or sudden death than those who stay calm in face of stress.

If you nearly burst a blood vessel when a shoelace breaks or believe that no-good deed goes unpunished, you may want to give some thought to changing your attitudes. They may be more damaging to your health than you think.

Just being aware that you get stressed easily is enough to begin modifying your behaviour.

See also: TAKE IT EASY; ARE MALES MORE AGGRESSIVE THAN FEMALES; GIVE YOURSELF TIME.

Break Free of the Yawn Circle

Isn't it just embarrassing to not be able to stop yawning? This is specially true when you are in situations where yawning can be interpreted as being bored.

There are several theories trying to explain why we yawn. But the fact is, we don't really know.

Staying glued to your desk for hours at a stretch is physically and mentally exhausting and leaves you, at times, so yawny and lethargic that you would rather go to sleep. The best way to beat this feeling is by giving yourself a break. A brisk five-minute walk is a perfect recipe to rev up and recharge your engine. You will return to work fully charged and refreshed.

Your yawning may be attributed to not getting enough sleep. Go to bed at an earlier time, keeping your room dark and cool and blocking out the light. If you don't get enough sleep you won't be able to stop yawning.

Try to take a nap during the day. If you work a 9-5 job, try to take naps on the weekends.

Exercising once a day will greatly increase your energy and prevent fatigue.

Don't eat too much at lunch. When you stuff yourself at lunch your body slows down while it processes everything you ate leading to tired and yawny afternoons. Eat a light lunch to stop yawning.

Eat more fruit. Cut out the sweets and the junk and eat a healthier diet. You are what you eat, and putting bad stuff in will make you feel tired faster.

See also: SLEEP LIKE A BABY; TO NAP OR NOT TO NAP.

Laugh — Life is Short

Study after study indicates that every belly laugh boosts your immune system's disease fighters for a short period of time. So, do your best to keep those immune system fighters at their peak by laughing as often as you can.

Laughter, along with an active sense of humour, may also help protect you against a heart attack, according to a 2008 study by cardiologists at the University of Maryland Medical Center in Baltimore. The study, which is the first to indicate that laughter may help prevent heart disease, found that people with heart disease were 40 per cent less likely to laugh in a variety of situations compared to people of the same age without heart disease.

'The old saying that "laughter is the best medicine," definitely appears to be true for protecting your heart,' says Prof. Michael Miller, director of the Center for Preventive Cardiology at the University of Maryland Medical Center. 'We don't know yet why laughing protects the heart, but we know that mental stress is associated with impairment of the protective barrier lining our blood vessels which can lead to fat and cholesterol build-up in the coronary arteries and ultimately to a heart attack.'

Says Miller, 'Recommendation for a healthy heart may one day be exercise, eat right and laugh a few times a day.'

And laughter appears to burn calories, too. Maciej Buchowski, a researcher from Vanderbilt University, USA, conducted a small study in which he measured the amount of calories expended in laughing. It turned out that 10-15 minutes of laughter burned 50 calories.

Feeling rundown? Try laughing more. Some researchers think laughter just might be *the* medicine, not only for putting that spring back in your step, but also for a healthier you.

Avoiding Conjunctivitis

Conjunctivitis, or pinkeye, refers to an inflammation of the conjunctiva, the thin transparent membrane covering the front of the eye. It spreads mostly through direct contact. Overcrowding, dirty surroundings and unhealthy living conditions can spread of this ailment.

Conjunctivitis results from bacterial or a virus infection. Other causes include allergic reactions, chemical or physical exposures, and ocular drying or irritation.

The common symptoms are itching under the eye lid, excessive watering, swelling of eye balls, eye lids getting glued while waking up, sensitivity to light, burning sensation and/or feeling of sand in the eyes.

Antibiotic eye drops or ointments maybe prescribed to reduce the swelling, redness, discomfort and to prevent any damage to the eye. Ocular decongestants, anti-allergy or anti-inflammatory medicines maybe used, if required.

Conjunctivitis is contagious. It is best to limit your contact with the outside world until you are better. If you have conjunctivitis carefully wash your hands every time you touch your face around the eye. Use tissue wipes and don't touch the infected eyes. Keep towels, wash cloths, and pillows separate from those of other family members. Even shared eye drops may cause the spread of infection.

Contacts, should not be worn and eye makeup discarded until the infection has fully gone.

Putting a cold compress, such as a wash cloth soaked in cold water, on the eye for a few minutes, eases discomfort and helps break up some of the crust that may form on the eyelashes.

Unfortunately, it takes about a week for conjunctivitis to go away. Be patient.

Learn Cancer's Warning Signs

Cancer may be 100 different diseases with a wide variety of causes, but you need to learn what the major warnings symptoms are. Early detection is the key to successful treatment and survival.

The most common forms of the disease are lung cancer, colon and rectal cancer, breast cancer, prostate cancer, cancer of the urinary tract and uterine cancer.

According to the American Cancer Society, the major warning signs are:

- A change in bowel or bladder habits.
- A lump or thickening in the breast, testicles or another body part.
- Obvious change in the size, colour, shape or thickness of wart, mole, or mouth sore.
- A sore that does not heal. Nagging cough or hoarseness.
- Indigestion or difficulty in swallowing.
- Unusual vaginal or rectal bleeding or discharge.
- Persistent headaches.
- Unexplained loss of weight or appetite.
- Chronic pain in bones or other areas of the body.
- Persistent fatigue, nausea, or vomiting.
- Persistent low-grade fever, either constant or intermittent.
- Repeated instances of infection.

If you have any of symptoms, see your physician as soon as possible. And if the symptoms are caused by cancer, early diagnosis and treatment is essential.

The greatest single truth about the cancer enigma is that most cancers, when detected and treated early, are curable.

Prime Your Pump

Day-after-day, year-after-year, your heart beats approximately 70 to 80 times every minute and 1,00,000 times a day. Every day, it pumps about 40,000 litres of blood through approximately 60,000 kilometres of blood vessels in your body. With every heartbeat, 300 *trillion* cells receive nourishment.

That's a lot of work. But your heart will keep working for a long time if you're good to it.

The American Heart Association has established some easy-to-follow guidelines to help reduce your risk of heart disease:

The simplest positive change to effectively improve your health is to start walking. It is enjoyable, free, easy and a great exercise. A walking programme is flexible and boasts high success rate. It is likely to become a regular and a satisfying part of your life.

At least 150 minutes of moderate exercise or 75 minutes of vigorous exercise per week is recommended. A 30 minutes a day capsule, fives times a week, is easy goal to remember and follow.

Eat a wide variety of foods, so your body will have a broad base of nutrients from which to meet its needs.

Limit alcohol consumption.

Keep your total fat intake under 30 per cent of your total daily calories.

Keep saturated and polyunsaturated fats under 10 per cent of total daily calories.

Get 50 per cent of your daily calories from complex carbohydrates such as pasta and potatoes. Keep cholesterol under 200 milligrams a day.

See also: TRY AN ANTI-AGEING PILL; ADOPT AN ESKIMO DIET; HOW DOES ASPIRIN BENEFIT THE HEART.

The Right Way to Stretch

The right way to stretch is slow and relaxed. But before stretching, take a few minutes to warm your muscles. Stretching muscles when they're cold increases the risk of injury, including pulled muscles. Warm up by walking while gently swinging your arms, or do a low-intensity exercise, such as walking, for at least five minutes.

Stretching techniques are fairly simple and easy to learn. Here are some guidelines to consider:

- When you begin a stretch, spend the first 15 seconds in an easy stretch. Stretch just until you feel a mild tension, then relax as you hold the stretch. The tension should be comfortable, not painful.
- Hold your stretches for at least 10 to 30 seconds and up to a minute for a really tight muscle or problem area. That can seem like a long time, so use a watch or count out loud to make sure you're holding your stretches long enough.
- Once you've completed the easy stretch, stretch just a fraction of centimetre farther until you again feel mild tension. Hold it for 15 seconds. Again, you should feel tension, but not pain.
- Relax and breathe freely while you're stretching. Try not to hold your breath. If you're bending forward to do a stretch, exhale as you bend forward and then breathe slowly as you hold the stretch.
- Avoid bouncing. This can actually cause you to pull the muscle you are trying to stretch. It can cause small tears in muscle, which leave scar tissue as the muscle heals. The scar tightens the muscle further, making you even less flexible, and more prone to pain.

- Avoid locking your joints. Bend your joints slightly while stretching.
- Each Stretching Session should last for about 10 to 20 minutes.
- To improve your performance in any sport or workout and to prevent injury, stretch before doing the workout routines or playing a sport.
- Avoid strenuous stretching for one to two hours after eating.
- During hot or humid days, do your strenuous stretching early morning or evening, when it is cooler or less humid.
- Don't stretch a muscle that you've recently injured, unless your doctor gives you a go signal. Still, try to use supports like wrist and knee wraps.
- You can stretch anytime you feel like it (e.g. at your desk,

waiting for a bus) and at various times of the day when you can.
- To maintain your flexibility, stretch at least three times a week.

Stretching is a mild, gentle activity. You don't need to push it. The benefits come from regularity. Stick with it and see how you feel in a few weeks.

See also: MINIMIZING EARLY MORNING BACKACHE; SPINE FLEXIBILITY TEST: IT'S EASY; TENSE YOUR MUSCLE TO RELAX.

Know What Painkillers to Take

Make sure you take painkillers properly, so you get the maximum effect.

Pain relievers are called analgesics (from the Greek words *an* meaning 'without' and '*algos*, meaning pain').

Each year, people spend billions of rupees to relieve acute or chronic pain associated with headache, cold, toothache, muscle ache, back ache, menstrual cramps etc. with over-the-counter analgesics. They include aspirin, acetaminophen, ibuprofen and sodium naproxen. All are effective at relieving mild to moderate pain and sometimes even severe pain; they work by stopping production of certain hormones in the nervous system which carry pain signals to the brain.

Popping pills to fight pain may seem an easy thing to do, but there are some important tips you should follow when using these drugs, whether they are prescription or over-the-counter (OTC). However, you should know that OTC analgesics are of two kinds: Those that decrease pain and also decrease inflammation and those that don't.

NSAIDs (nonsteriod anti-inflammatory drugs) are helpful when inflammation is present with the pain, e.g some forms of arthritis. Acetaminophen doesn't relieve inflammation and is relatively free of side-effects and therefore maybe a good alternative for long-term use as against NSAIDs.

For using pain medications safely at home, follow the following guidelines:

First, always use the weakest painkiller you can to fight pain.

Second, take the analgesic on a fixed schedule. This makes it easier to control the pain.

Third, take the recommended dosage, so you maintain a

constant level of the drug in your blood system. Never use more than the maximal recommended dose.

Fourth, use your medication to 'stay ahead' of your pain and keep it controlled. In this way, you can avoid the need for higher dosages or stronger drugs.

Fifth, unless a doctor recommends it, adults should not use pain medication for more than 10 days consecutively. The limit for children and teenagers is 5 days.

Sixth, take NSAIDs with milk and food to help minimize stomach upset.

Seventh, don't take aspirin during the last 3 months of pregnancy unless your doctor recommends it. Aspirin can cause bleeding in both the mother and child. Children should not take aspirin unless directed to do so by a physician.

Eight, if you are allergic to aspirin, check with your doctor about which pain relievers you can use safely.

Ninth, avoid alcohol. Mixing alcohol with aspirin, ibuprofen or naproxen sodium increases the chance of stomach upset and bleeding.

If you have any doubts about the impact of any painkiller on you, speak to your doctor candidly or look up a good reference book. There may be effective alternatives.

See also: HOW MANY KINDS OF PAIN ARE THERE?; USE ANTIBIOTICS ONLY FOR BACTERIAL INFECTIONS.

Make a Personal Health Plan

Making a personal health plan that outlines what you do to stay healthy can help you take control of your health.

Use a blank book, a spiral-bound book, a ring binder or any other convenient format to record your plan. The following are some of the items you may want to keep track of:

Medications: what you take and when to take.

Exercise schedule: what exercises you engage in and when.

Relaxation exercise schedule: what relaxation techniques you use and when.

Healthy habits you're working on, such as eating more vegetables and walking.

Important phone numbers: your nearest family member(s) and/or friend(s), your doctor, nearest hospital with emergency care facilities, pharmacist, therapist and any health organizations that are important to you.

Questions for your doctor.

A written health plan can prove invaluable because it keeps you on track and thinking about your health.

See also: USE A SECURITY BLANKET.

Discourage Gallstones

Millions of people, mostly women, get gallstones, and many experience severe pain. Sometimes even surgery is required.

The most common kind of gallstone is made of cholesterol — the same fat that can clog your arteries and cause heart disease. A genetic error in cholesterol metabolism may make certain people more susceptible to gallstone formation. Being female, overweight, diabetic or having a family history of gallstones are all major risk factors that increase your chances of getting them.

You can't do much about your family or your gender, but you can reduce your risk of developing this potentially serious problem by exercising regularly to keep your weight down and by eating a diet that is rich in fibre (foods such as fresh vegetables, fruits and whole grains), consuming less dietary fat and avoiding foods that are high in sugar or refined carbohydrates especially bakery products.

Majority of gallstones do not cause a symptom. The most common symptoms of gallstones are billiary colic.

While it isn't easy to build healthy diet and regular exercise in your daily routine, it is the best thing you can do to prevent gallstones.

See also: STOP BELLYACHING; WHEN STOMACH DISAGREES.

Aerobic versus Anaerobic Exercise

Aerobic and anaerobic exercises form essential parts of a fitness regimen. Both contribute in maintaining overall health of the person.

Aerobic exercise (which literally means 'to exercise with oxygen') occurs when you continuously move large muscle groups such as leg muscles. This exercise places increased demands on the heart, lungs and muscle cells. It is not so intense, however, that it causes pain. If you're exercising in a good aerobic range, you should be sweating and breathing faster but still be able to exercise comfortably for 20 to 40 minutes. Such exercise improves overall endurance. Walking, biking, jogging and swimming are familiar examples of aerobic exercises.

Anaerobic exercise ('to exercise without oxygen') occurs when the demands made on a muscle are great enough that it uses up all of the available oxygen and starts to burn stored energy without oxygen. This alternate path for burning energy produces lactic acid. As lactic acid builds up in muscles it causes pain. That's one reason why you can't carry on anaerobic exercises very long. Weight lifting and stress training workouts are classic examples of such activity.

Anaerobic exercise are helpful in building strength but not endurance. It uses resistance for building muscle and bone. Aerobic exercise will have more of an impact on the cardiovascular and circulatory system.

If you are just starting an exercise program, supplement your aerobic exercises with light anaerobic exercises. Work with light weights or set machines at light resistance to avoid injuries. This way you can increase muscle mass, burn fat and get more oxygen into your body. All of these will make you healthier.

Myths About Allergy

Allergies often seem vague in origin and unpredictable in response. So it's not surprising that several misconceptions about their causes and cure exist. The common myths about allergies are described below:

Allergies are psychosomatic. Although hay fever affects your eyes and nose, allergies aren't 'all in your head.' An allergy is a real medical condition involving your immune system. Stress or emotions may bring on or worsen symptoms, but emotions don't cause allergies.

Moving to dry climate will cure allergies. Some people who are bothered by allergies to pollens and moulds believe moving to arid areas, where the foliage and climate are different, will cause their allergies to disappear. The desert may lack some of the trees and weeds that may have made things difficult, but it does have other plants that can produce pollen. People who are sensitive to some pollens and moulds may become sensitive to the pollens and moulds found in new environments.

Short-haired pets don't cause allergies. An animal's fur (regardless of its length) isn't the culprit in allergies. The cause is the dander and sometimes saliva and urine. If you're allergic to furry pets, safer pets include fish and reptiles.

Organic food are non-allergenic. Limiting your diet to organic food is no guarantee that you will avoid food allergy. Some of the most allergenic foods are 'natural' foods — cow's milk, eggs, peanuts, wheat, soya beans, fish and nuts. Allergies are caused not by chemicals but by proteins in the food.

See also: DRUG ALLERGIES; CONTROL ALLERGY ATTACKS; FIGHT INTOLERANCE.

The Alternate Nostril Breathing Technique

Oxygen is the most vital nutrient for our body. It is essential for the integrity of the brain, nerves, glands and internal organs.

The exercise explained below has its origin in the fourth part of the eight fold yoga described in *Yogasutra* of Patanjali and is called Anuloma Viloma. It is designed to increase the supply of oxygen to the body. It restores the normal breathing pattern between nostrils and raises our health and vitality levels.

With this exercise, we breathe through only one nostril at a time. This exercise follows the natural normal breathing pattern which alternates from one nostril to the other at various times during the day. You can easily prove this to yourself. Just squeeze one nostril closed with your thumb and try breathing through just the one nostril. Repeat this procedure with the other nostril. You'll find it much easier to breathe through one of the nostrils than the other. One of the nostrils will always be partially blocked; we are always breathing mainly through one nostril.

In a healthy person the breath will alternate between nostrils about every two hours. Because most of us are not in optimum health, this time period varies considerably between people and further reduces our vitality.

According to yoga, when the breath continues to flow in one nostril for more than two hours, as it does with most of us, it has an adverse effect on our health. If the right nostril is involved, the result is mental and nervous disturbance. If the left nostril is involved, the result is chronic fatigue and reduced brain function. The longer the flow of breath in one nostril, the more serious the illness will be.

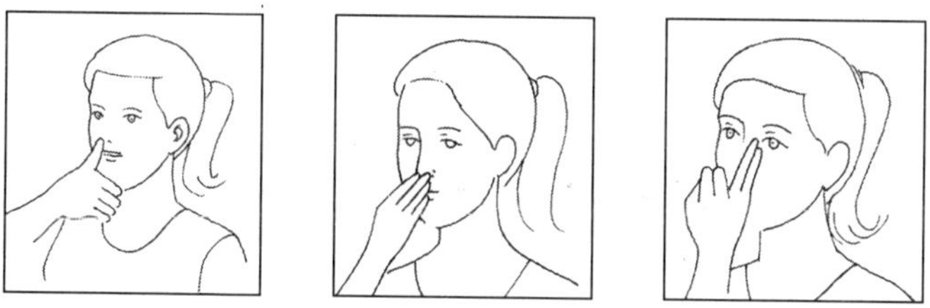

Exercise

- Close the right nostril with your right thumb and inhale through the left nostril. Do this to the count of four seconds.
- Immediately close the left nostril with your right ring finger and little finger, and at the same time remove your thumb from the right nostril, and exhale through this nostril. Do this to the count of eight seconds. This completes a half round.
- Inhale through the right nostril to the count of four seconds. Close the right nostril with your right thumb and exhale through the left nostril to the count of eight seconds. This completes one full round.
- Start by doing three rounds, adding one per week until you are doing seven rounds.

The alternate nostril breathing exercise produces optimum function on both sides of the brain: that is optimum creativity and optimum logical verbal activity. It also creates a more balanced person, with both halves of the brain functioning properly. Yoga considers this to be the best technique to calm the mind and the nervous system.

See also: TRY AN 'ANTI-AGEING' PILL.

Motion Sickness

Any type of transport can cause motion sickness. It can strike suddenly, progressing from a feeling of restlessness to a cold sweat, dizziness and then vomiting and diarrhoea. Motion sickness usually quieten down as soon as the motion stops. The more you travel, the more easily you'll adjust to being in motion.

You can plan ahead to escape motion sickness with the help of following tips:

- Focus on the horizon or a distant, stationary object.
- Don't read.
- Don't overeat. Avoid spicy foods and alcohol.
- Take an over-the-counter antihistamine such as meclizine or dimenhydrinate before you feel sick. Expect drowsiness as a side effect.
- Many medicines such as Promethazine (*Avomine*) are available on a doctor's prescription which when taken one hour before you're in motion, offer protection for the next 8 to 12 hours. You must, however, avoid using the medication if you have health problems such as glaucoma, or urine retention.
- If you become ill, eating dry crackers or drinking a carbonated beverage may help settle your stomach.
- If you're on a plane, ask for a seat over the front edge of a wing. Once aboard, direct the air vent at your face. On a train, take a seat near a window, and face forward. In an automobile, drive or sit in the front passenger's seat. Keep your head still, rested against a seat back.
- Don't smoke or sit near smokers.

Home Medical Supplies

When an emergency or medical problem occurs in the home, you often don't have time to search for supplies. Keep your medical supplies in a place that is easily accessible to adults but not children.

Here's what you need to be properly prepared for accidents and common illnesses:

For cuts: Bandages of various sizes, gauze, adhesive tape, an antiseptic solution to clean wounds and an antiseptic cream to prevent infection.

For burns: Cold packs, gauze, burn spray and an antiseptic cream.

For aches, pain and fever: Aspirin (for adults only) or another nonsteroidal anti-inflammatory drug, and acetaminophen for children or adults.

For eye injuries: Eyewash, an eyewash cup and eye patches.

For sprains, strains and fractures: Cold packs, elastic wraps for wrapping injuries and a triangular bandage for making an arm sling.

For insect bites and stings: A tweezer to remove stings and hydrocortisone cream to relieve itching.

For general care: Thermometer, sharp scissors, cottons swabs, tissues, soap or cleansing pads, and a first aid manual.

And, finally, remember to replace items after their use to make sure the kit is always complete.

See also: CLEAN OUT YOUR MEDICINE CABINET; KNOW WHAT PAINKILLERS TO TAKE; LEARN HOW TO TAKE TEMPERATURE.

When You Shouldn't 'Wait and See'

Oftentimes, when a particular sign or symptom develops, our natural response is to wait a day or two and see if it goes away. In many instances, such as if you develop a sore throat or experience back pain after a day of lifting, this approach is OK. But certain signs and symptoms demand an immediate response. Seek emergency medical care if you experience any of the following:

- Uncontrolled bleeding
- Difficulty in breathing or shortness of breath
- Severe chest or upper abdominal pain or pressure
- Fainting, sudden dizziness or weakness
- Weakening or numbness of an arm
- Sudden, marked change in vision
- Confusion or changes in mental state
- Any sudden or severe pain
- Severe or persistent vomiting or diarrhoea
- Coughing or vomiting blood
- Suicidal or homicidal feelings

You may also have other warning signs to be aware of, based on your personal medical history.

See also: LEARN THE WARNING SIGNS OF DIABETES; HOW MANY KINDS OF PAIN ARE THERE?; MAKE A PERSONAL HEALTH PLAN; LEARN CANCER'S WARNING SIGNS.

Eat Your Colours

The idea that a healthy plate of food will feature several different colours is a good example of an old wives' tale being good science.

The colours of many vegetables reflect the different antioxidant phytochemicals they contain — anthocyanins, polyphenols, flavonoids, carotenoids. Many of these chemicals help protect against chronic diseases, but each in a slightly different way, so the best protection comes from a diet containing as many different phytochemicals as possible.

'Colourful food not only lowers cancer risk but also prevents ageing process,' says Dr. Nagi Kumar of Moffitt Cancer Centre & Research Institute, University of South Florida College of Medicine. Specific nutrients have specific colours. The deeper the colour of a food, the more of that kind of nutrients it has.

Red is rich in lycopene which reduces cancer risks — tomatoes, watermelons, grapes, strawberries, red apples.

Orange contain alpha and beta carotene to improve cell-to-cell communication and slow cancer — carrots, mangoes, sweet potatoes.

Orange/Yellow contain Vitamin C which protects cells — oranges, papayas.

Yellow/Green are rich sources of carotenoids lutein and zeaxanthin which contribute to eye health — spinach, corn, green peas, avocados.

Green contain sulforaphane which stimulates liver genes to make compounds that breakdown cancer-causing chemicals — broccoli, cabbage.

White/Green contain flavonoids that protect cell membranes — onions, garlic, pears.

If you want to live well, you have to eat well.

The Whiter the Bread, the Sooner You'll be Dead

This rather blunt bit of cross-cultural grandmotherly advice suggests that the health risks of white flour have been popularly recognized for previous three or four generations.

As far as the body is concerned, white flour is not much different from sugar. Unless supplemented, it offers none of the good things (fibre, B vitamins, healthy fats) that whole grains offer — it's little more than a shot of glucose. Large spikes of glucose are inflammatory and wreak havoc on our insulin metabolism. White bread is made from wheat flour from which the bran and the germ have been removed.

Eat whole grains and minimize your consumption of white flour. For example, whole wheat bread is much higher in fibre than white bread. Fibre aids digestion, helps you feel full and reduces the risk of heart attacks and strokes.

See also: EAT YOUR COLOURS; FEAST ON FIBRE.

Pay Attention to Floor Safety

Most people feel secure and safe at home. Yet thousands of people are killed in home accidents each year, and many more suffer serious injuries that are treated at hospitals; some people are unfortunately, even disabled.

Many of these tragic accidents are falls that are due to hazards that are easy to overlook, but equally easy to fix.

If you have carpets on the floor keep them smooth — even a small wrinkle can cause someone to trip. And if you notice that the corners of the carpet are curling, secure them with carpet tape. Possibly the safest option is to use carpets with non-slip backing.

Tape or fix all loose wires and cords — telephone or extension cords, lamp wires etc. — to the wall so that no one can trip over them. If necessary, call an electrician to do so. Never run electrical wires under the carpet. Electrical wires can dry out or fray and need replacement. You can't see what condition they're in when they're hidden under carpet. Also, don't run wires across 'lanes' where people walk.

If you have a staircase at home it should have a two-way light switch both at the top and bottom of the staircase. Also remember to have the staircase always well-lit, day or night. The fall you prevent might be your own!

See also: PRACTICE KITCHEN CAUTION.

Give Yourself Time

In our society, with its instant coffee, instant political polls and instant electronic communication, we are becoming too impatient. Parents, children, spouses, employers and employees all lose patience with each other.

The important things in life — birth, growth, love, friendship, health and healing — all take time and require

patience. You can't force a flower to grow, a child to mature, a love to blossom or a wound to heal.

But if you're patient, your life will unfold before you. Maybe not exactly as you had planned or wished it to be, but perhaps even more beautifully than you could have imagined.

When you feel impatient, take a moment to quietly sit and slowly breathe in and out. Let your body relax. The peacefulness that comes with patience will provide a strong foundation for a healthy you.

It may help you to say to yourself, 'I have right to savour this moment,' or 'there are always problems, but here and now I'm doing just fine.'

When you are feeling good, you maybe able to feel even better. Just experiment with allowing unnecessary tension to fade, and allow satisfaction to fill you up inside. In good time or tough, keep letting go, and enjoy each shift of life's kaleidoscope.

See also: GO WHERE YOU'VE NEVER GONE BEFORE; CHERISH YOUR FRIENDS.

Learn How to Take Temperature

Your body temperature fluctuates throughout the day. But if your temperature is over 99° F (as measured by an oral thermometer), it's safe to assume you have a fever.

The fever thermometer is the second most frequently used test after hand on the forehead, to judge fever. Several types of thermometers are available: glass thermometers, electronic thermometers and tymphanic (ear) thermometers. Disposable temperature strips are also available but are often inaccurate.

Reading an oral thermometer takes practice. The following will help you read the thermometer accurately:

Prepare a glass thermometer by cleaning it with clean, cool water or alcohol, or by holding it firmly between two fingers and flicking your wrist to shake the indicator to less than 98.6° F (37° C) and ideally down to 92° F.

Then place the bulb under the tongue and close the mouth for 3 minutes. Remove the thermometer and rotate until you can read the temperature.

Oral thermometer can also be used for an armpit reading. Keep the thermometer for 5 minutes and add 1° to the reading to convert to an approximate oral temperature.

Overlooking simple things can cause inaccurate readings. If you use an oral thermometer shortly after drinking a hot liquid or too soon after exercising, for example, you may get a high reading without any fever at all. Women's temperature can be affected by hormonal changes, such as those that occur around ovulation.

To ensure an accurate reading, sit down and avoid eating or drinking anything for at least fifteen minutes before taking temperature.

Drug Allergies

Almost any drug can cause an adverse reaction in some people. Reactions to most drugs are not common, but they can range from merely irritating to life-threatening. Symptoms of allergic reactions to drugs include wheezing and difficulty in breathing, rash, hives, generalized itching and shock. Some reactions (such as rashes) are true allergic responses. Most, however, are side-effects of a particular drug, typified by dry mouth or fatigue. Your physician will determine the nature of the reactions and what to do about them.

Penicillin and its relatives are responsible for many drug allergy reactions, ranging from mild rashes to hives to immediate anaphylaxis. Most reactions are minor rashes.

Drugs most likely to cause reactions include sulfas, barbiturates, anticonvulsants, insulin and local anaesthetics. These are all common, effective, useful medications. If you're taking one of them and not having problems, don't stop using it. In addition, contrast dyes in some X-ray studies to help outline major organs contain iodine and may cause an allergic reaction.

Millions of people primarily adults, have reactions to aspirin. Although not a true allergy, the response mimics one, and it can be serious.

The most common drug reactions — rash, itching and hives — are treated with antihistamines or, occasionally, cortisone. Most drug allergies cannot be cured; penicillin allergy being an exception. In some case, this sensitivity can be reduced enough so that the person can tolerate the drug. Small amounts of the drug are given in slowly increasing amounts to desensitize the immune response.

Dry Eyes and Watery Eyes

Dry eye syndrome is a chronic lack of sufficient lubrication and moisture on the surface of the eye. Oddly enough, one of the most common causes of watery eyes or excess tearing is dry eyes. One of the main tests for excess tearing is to check whether the eyes are too dry.

Tear production decreases as we age and tends to affect post-menopausal women more. Dry eyes usually affect both the eyes; eyes feel hot, irritated, gritty to blink and may become slightly red. Some medicines (such as sleeping medicines, antihistamines and some medicines for high blood pressure) can cause or worsen dry eyes.

As a thumb rule over-the-counter eye drops should not be used for more than 3 to 5 days because they can cause dry eyes.

Hair dryers (or other sources of air such as car heaters or fans) should not be directed toward the eyes.

Wear glasses on windy days and goggles when swimming to protect the eyes.

Using a preservative-free artificial tear preparation lessens dryness but seek medical care if the condition persists.

Your eyes may actually water in response to dryness and irritation and lead to watery eyes. Excessive watering can result from infections, or allergic reaction to preservatives in eye drops or contact lens solutions. Watery eyes also can result from a blockage in the ducts that drain tears to the inside of your nose. Overflow tears can cause even more eye irritation and tearing.

Don't rub your eyes. Applying a warm compress over closed eyelids two to four times a day for 10 minutes provides relief.

See also: AVOIDING CONJUNCTIVITIS.

Painful Menses

Most women are familiar with menstrual cramps. During menstruation, you may feel pain in the lower abdomen, possibly extending to the hips, lower back or thighs. Some women also have nausea, vomiting, diarrhoea or general aching. It is normal to have mild abdominal cramps on the first day or two of your period (more than half of women do). However, about 10 per cent of women experience pain so severe that they can't manage their normal routine unless they take medication.

If there is no underlying gynaecological disorder, the pain is called primary dysmenorrhoea. It may be due to fibroid tumour (a benign tumour in the wall of your uterus), a sexually transmitted disease, endometriosis, pelvic inflammatory disease or an ovarian cyst or tumour.

Talk to your doctor if the menstrual pain is severe or is associated with fever; if you have unusual nausea, vomiting or abdominal pain; or if the pain lasts beyond the third day of menstrual flow.

Treatment of the underlying cause should relieve the pain.

Nonsteroidal anti-inflammatory drugs or aspirin relieves pain in about 80 per cent of women.

Many women find soaking in a warm tub or exercising helps ease their pain.

See also: BREAST TENDERNESS; WOMEN: CHECK YOUR BREASTS; EDUCATE YOURSELF ON MAMMOGRAPHY.

Preventing Heat Stroke

Heat stroke or sun stroke occurs when a person's core body temperature increases above the relatively safe levels of 102°-103° F. Heat stroke is a medical emergency and can be fatal if not promptly and properly treated. Infants, elderly, athletes and outdoor workers are at greatest risk of heat stroke.

Heat cramps or painful muscle spasms are early signs of impending heat stroke. Heat exhaustion can occur rapidly and turn life-threatening. Signs of heat exhaustion include high temperature, faintness, low blood pressure, an ashen appearance, cold, clammy skin and nausea. Other signs are small pupils, a rapid but weak pulse and shallow breathing.

Symptoms can often begin suddenly, sometimes after excessive perspiration and inadequate fluid intake. Cooling the victim is a critical step in the treatment of heat stroke.

If untreated, heat stroke can result in shock, brain damage or even death.

To prevent heat stroke drinking plenty of clean, cool water, avoiding prolonged exposure to intense heat and application of cool wet towel to your skin frequently is recommended. It is best to avoid exhausting activity if your body is not well-conditioned. If possible stay indoors or in the shade.

Unless absolutely essential heavy exertion and exercising in hot weather should be avoided or scheduled for cooler part of the day with frequent rest intervals. Eating regular, light meals and wearing loose fitting light-weight clothing is advised.

The best defence is prevention. Don't wait until you are thirsty to drink. Drink more fluids, regardless of your activity level in hot weather.

Is Your Brain a Computer?

The human brain is much more than a computer. No computer can decide that it is bored or wasting its talents and embark on a new way of life. A computer cannot drastically alter its own program; a person with a brain must reprogram it.

While a computer processes information a single step at a time, the brain, with its trillions of cross-linked neural connections, processes information along millions of multidirectional pathways simultaneously. Both a computer and a brain are equipped with electricity-powered mechanisms for storing, retrieving, and processing information. Does all this make the brain a computer? In this limited sense, yes.

But a computer cannot relax, or daydream, or laugh. It cannot become inspired or creative. It cannot experience consciousness or perceive meaning. It cannot fall in love. Once more, then — is the brain a computer? In a word, no. Language and abstract thought, judgement and planning, advanced reasoning and learning, all of these would be impossible without the highly developed human brain. But the brain is much, much more than the centre of intellectual activity. You need your brain to breathe, to metabolize food, and even to excrete wastes. The brain regulates and coordinates all the voluntary and involuntary moves you make, all the sensory impressions you receive, all the emotions you feel.

In short, your brain is what makes you human. The Greek physician Hippocrates recognized as much in the 5th century BC, when he observed what happened to people with head wounds. 'From the brain and from the brain only,' he said, 'arise our pleasures, joys, laughter, and jets as well as our sorrows, pains, griefs, and fears.'

Lifting Properly

Everyone should learn how to lift loads; all of us lift loads almost every day of our life, for example — a piece of luggage, laundry basket, a piece of furniture which we want to shift — the list is endless.

Improper lifting technique can lead to back, leg and arm pain. Poor technique can cause both acute injury and serious chronic effects. Learning the right way to lift will help you avoid these problems. Follow these steps:

1. Position your feet firmly, toes pointed slightly outward, one foot slightly ahead of the other. Stand as close to the load as possible.
2. Bend from your knees, and use your powerful leg muscles to lift the load. Keep your back as upright as possible. As you lift, tighten the abdominal muscles that support your spine.
3. Hold the load close to your body. Avoid turning or twisting while holding the load. Avoid lifting heavy loads above your waist.

Always think through your task before you begin lifting and ask for assistance when you need it, as experts sensibly advise.

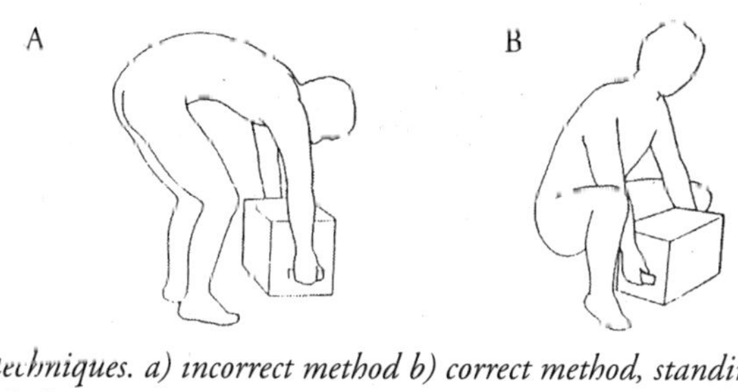

Lifting techniques. a) incorrect method b) correct method, standing close to the load with the spine straight and the feet firmly balanced.

Unexpected Weight Changes

In most cases, the reasons for change in weight are obvious. Changes in diet or activity are the usual explanations. However, physical illness also can effect your weight. An unexpected weight change of 5 to 10 per cent of your weight in six or fewer months is significant. If you lose or gain weight and can't point to a reason, talk to your doctor.

Weight gain is the most common scenario in adulthood. It usually creeps up gradually — a few kilograms a year. Careful diet and regular exercise can stop this trend. If you've experienced a rapid gain, consider these possible causes:

Diet changes — increased intake of alcohol or soda, a new favourite high-fat food such as ice creams, sweets, fried foods, increased snacking, a switch to fast foods.

Decrease in activity — an injury restricting movement, a switch from an active to a sedentary job or a change in a routine such as using stairs or walking to work.

New medication — some medicines may contribute to weight gain.

Changes in mood — excessive anxiety, stress or depression can affect activity and food intake.

Fluid retention — if you have noticed puffiness of the tissues, tightening of rings or shoes, swelling of the ankles as the day progresses, unusual shortness of breath or new, frequent trips to the bathroom at night consult your doctor.

If changes in diet or decrease in activity apply to you, change your diet and increase your activity. Wait four to six weeks to see if the changes work. If they don't affect your weight, or if new medication, mood changes or fluid retention applies to you then see your doctor.

Weight Loss. Unexplained weight loss of 5 to 10 per cent of your body weight over six or fewer months is usually cause for concern.

Change in diet — skipping meals, a significant reduction in fat intake, a change in meal preparation methods, a change in routines around meal time, eating alone.

Change in activity — change, to an active job, new exercise program, hectic schedule, seasonal variation.

Mood changes — anxiety, stress and depression also can cause weight loss.

Other conditions — dental problems, uncontrolled diabetes with thirst or increased urination; hyperthyroidism (over active thyroid gland); digestive disorders such as malabsorption or ulcer with abdominal pain; inflammatory bowel diseases, such as intestinal tuberculosis; cancer of many types.

If changes in diet or activity apply to you, but none of the other items seem to fit, modify your diet. Eat three balanced meals. For snacks, or when you can't eat a good meal, try a nutritional supplement drink. Instant breakfasts are simple, fairly balanced and less expensive than prepared supplements. If you haven't reversed the weight loss trend in two weeks, or if you suspect some other reason, perhaps a new medicine you are taking, consult your doctor without delay.

Kids' Care

Weight loss or failure to grow in children may be caused by a digestive problem that prevents important nutrients from being digested or absorbed. Loss of these nutrients can lead to bony changes and other problems. Your child also may have an eating disorder. If your child has unexplained weight loss, consult your child's health care provider.

Balance as You Age

A leading concern amongst the elderly is the apprehension of injury due to fall resulting from progressive impairment of ability to balance. Balance is associated with sensory input from the eyes, the correct functioning of the balance system of the inner ear, and the sense of position and movement in the feet, legs, and arms (the vestibular system).

Balance is also dependent on muscle strength and joint mobility. As we grow older we can improve our overall health and fitness, and specifically balance, by participating in low-impact sports, such as aerobics, yoga, tai chi, pilates, or water aerobics. Any activity that requires good body awareness, hand-eye coordination, and swaying movements can help sharpen balance skills.

The American Seniors Fitness Association recommends knee lifts exercise to improve balance. Attempt to lift the knee as high as the hip holding a secure object to assist in maintaining balance in the beginning. Try holding the leg up for 3 seconds or longer. It is important not to close your eyes due to difficulties maintaining balance.

While holding onto a wall, chair or the kitchen sink, raise yourself up and down on tiptoes, repeatedly. As your strength improves, go higher up on your toes and eventually try it on one foot at a time.

You can also practice balancing throughout the day. Practice standing on one leg while waiting in a queue or doing housework, or rise on your toes while washing the dishes or ironing and remember to take extra trips up and down the stairs. This strengthens your hips and thighs.

Breast Tenderness

During the week before a menstrual period, tenderness in both breasts is common. Tenderness can be due to premenstrual syndrome, birth control pills, pregnancy, or breast-feeding. Exercises such as jogging and aerobics can also cause breast tenderness.

Trim fat from your diet, recommend the health care providers. A diet that's high in fat isn't only bad for your heart — it can increase breast pain, as well. Experts believe that eating large amounts of fat can interfere with the production of chemicals in the body that are responsible for reducing breast pain. In addition, dietary fat has a way of turning into body fat, and fatty tissue has been shown to interfere with the body's ability to regulate estrogen.

Doctors recommend getting no more than 20 to 25 per cent of your total daily calories from fat. The best way to reduce fat in your diet is to cut back on the worst offenders — high-fat foods such as mayonnaise, red meats, margarine, butter, ice cream, and cheeses.

Avoiding caffeine, reducing salt and sugar in your diet before period, wearing a comfortable and supportive bra or taking an over-the-counter pain reliever are all helpful steps.

If the tenderness persists, consult your doctor.

See also: PAINFUL MENSES; WOMEN: CHECK YOUR BREASTS; EDUCATE YOURSELF ON MAMMOGRAPHY.

How Does Aspirin Benefit the Heart?

For over a hundred years aspirin has been used as a pain reliever. Since the 1970s it has also been used to prevent and manage heart disease. Research has shown that regular aspirin use is associated with a marked reduction from death particularly among the elderly, people with heart disease, and those physically unfit.

Aspirin benefits the heart in several ways. It decreases pain and inflammation associated with heart disease by blocking the action of an enzyme called prostaglandins (a kind of unsaturated fatty acids) which produces a chemical that signals an injury and triggers pain. By inhibiting prostaglandins, aspirin inhibits the formation of blood clots. Blood clots are harmful because they can clog the arteries leading to the heart, increasing the risk of heart attack and stroke.

Always speak to your doctor about the benefits and risks of aspirin before beginning a regular regimen. Recent research indicates an appropriate dose of aspirin for adults is between 80 and 160 mg per day. Many studies show the lower dose works just as well as the higher dose, while reducing the risk of internal bleeding. But it is best to check with your doctor to find out what is right dose for you.

People with coronary artery disease or atherosclerosis anywhere in the body (such as the brain or legs) angina, stents, peripheral artery disease (poor circulation) and bypass surgery are likely to benefit from aspirin therapy as also people who have had a transient ischemic attack (TIA) or ischemic stroke.

Persons who have no signs or symptoms but have an increased risk of first heart attack e.g. due to diabetes or other risk factors are likely to benefit from aspirin therapy. In general, people with a higher risk of heart attack have a greater potential for benefit.

In addition to your doctor's advise, it is helpful to follow the following guidelines:

Aspirin should not be taken on an empty stomach. It is advisable to take aspirin with a glass of water with meals or after meals to prevent stomach upset. The other important thing to remember is that aspirin is available both in chewable and non-chewable form. Never break, crush or chew extended-release tablets or capsules — swallow them whole. Chewable aspirin tablets may be chewed, crushed, or dissolved in a liquid.

Before taking aspirin prescribed by your doctor, tell him if you are allergic to aspirin, ibuprofen, or naproxen. Also remember to ask which other medicines you may take for pain relief or minor colds.

Caution

Aspirin should never be taken in place of other medications or treatments. Aspirin therapy should always be an adjunct and never an alternative to the management of other risk factors.

Although aspirin can greatly reduce the risk of a heart attack because it thins the blood, it also may slightly increase the risk of a bleeding stroke (haemorrhagic stroke). Daily aspirin use tends to increase the risk of developing a stomach ulcer; in person having a bleeding ulcer, aspirin will increase the bleeding, possibly to life threatening extent. Therefore, it is best to discuss with your doctor and weigh the pros and the cons of using aspirin in view of your health history.

The Food Drug Administrations of USA also warns that people who regularly take aspirin should limit the amount of alcohol they take because of its additional blood thinning effects and potential to upset the stomach.

See also: NEVER MIX ASPIRIN WITH VITAMIN C; DON'T GIVE ASPIRIN TO A CHILD WITH A FEVER.

Smoking: Its Never too Late to Stop

If you are a smoker, you don't need another sermon; instead here is some positive encouragement.

Whatever your reason for continuing to smoke, it's never too late to stop. Even if you don't quit until late in life, doing so has proven health benefits.

When you inhale tobacco smoke, you're ingesting a noxious combination of more than 4,000 toxic chemicals, including 63 carcinogens and trace amounts of several poisons.

Smoking is the cause of 87 per cent of all lung cancers — the most deadly form of cancer. It is a major risk factor for cancers of the mouth, larynx, pharynx, oesophagus, stomach, pancreas, kidney, bladder and cervix.

Tobacco smoke damages or destroys tiny air sacs in the lungs called alveoli. More than 80 per cent of deaths from chronic obstructive pulmonary disease are related to cigarette smoking.

The nicotine in tobacco triggers adrenal glands to produce hormones that increase blood pressure and heart rate. Smoking also contributes to the buildup of fatty deposits in the arteries (atherosclerosis). At the same time, the carbon monoxide in tobacco smoke binds to haemoglobin in the blood, taking the place of valuable oxygen and reducing the amount of oxygen available to the heart and other vital organs. All these increase the risk of heart attack and stroke.

Smoking increases your risk of respiratory infections, gum disease, cataracts, and peptic ulcers. In men, it increases the risk of erectile dysfunction. In postmenopausal women, it increases the risk of osteoporosis and hip fracture.

'But if I am in good health, active and enjoy a smoke, why should I give up?' is the logic smokers put forward. Why indeed? Here are some convincing benefits:

When you stop smoking, your health will improve almost immediately; the level of carbon

'Smoking won't kill you, but you'll cough for eternity!'

monoxide and nicotine in your system will decrease significantly. Within a few days, your senses of smell and taste should improve. You may breathe easier, and your smoker's cough will begin to disappear.

By the end of your first nonsmoking year, your risk of heart attack will decrease by half, and by five years it'll be almost the same as that of someone who has never smoked. Within seven years, your risk of bladder cancer will drop to that of a nonsmoker. And after 10 to 15 years of not smoking, your statistical risk of getting cancer of the lung, larynx or mouth will approach that of someone who has never smoked.

You'll also rid yourself of the unpleasantness associated with smoking — bad breath, yellow teeth and smelly clothing and hair. And you'll set the right example for your children, grandchildren and friends.

See also: BREAK ONE UNHEALTHY HABIT; QUICK FIXERS OR STRESS ENHANCERS.

Diarrhoea: Nature is the Answer

Diarrhoea is often a symptom of an infection or a long-term condition.

Common symptoms associated with diarrhoea are cramping stomach pains, an urgent need to go to the toilet, nausea or vomiting, fever and headache.

Most important thing in diarrhoea is to replenish the lost body water and electrolytes, and not allow yourself to get dehydrated. Taking clear liquids for the first 24 hours is advised. You may take *chhach, neembu pani, sherbat, daal ka pani, chawal ka maand,* green coconut water and similar other homely fluids. The easiest way is to buy a commercially available sachet of oral rehydration salts (ORS). Mix as per instructions and drink sufficient amount of it to maintain hydration level.

Washing hands regularly with soap and hot water helps in prevention and spread of diarrhoea. Washing your hands after using the toilet, playing with pets, and before touching food is particularly important. Teach children to wash their hands properly as soon as they are old enough to understand. Prevent germs from spreading by cleaning toilets with disinfectant and not sharing towels.

See also: HANDWASHING: THE WHY AND THE HOW; DO BACTERIA IN YOUR DIGESTIVE TRACT HURT YOU; UNDERSTANDING FOOD POISONING.

Use Antibiotics only for Bacterial Infections

Antibiotics, also known as antibacterials, are commonly used drugs to treat infections caused by bacteria. They are not effective against viruses.

There has been a dramatic increase in bacteria that are resistant to antibiotics. As a result, these bacteria can cause serious and sometimes fatal diseases such as pneumonia and meningitis.

Researchers from Barcelona to Atlanta, Switzerland to India, USA to Australia have reported that the rise in antibiotic-resistant bacteria is due to inappropriate use of antibiotics. They have found that instead of being prescribed exclusively for bacterial infections, the anti-bacteria drugs are being handed out to treat most upper respiratory tract infections, such as the common cold and sore throats, which are generally caused by viruses — antibiotics do not work against these viruses.

The result? Less than twenty years ago, penicillin-resistant bacteria were found in less than one per cent of people studied. Researchers estimate that today, there is a high percentage of adults who have infections resistant to penicillin.

The next time your doctor prescribes antibiotics, do ask if they're really necessary. A hot soup may be better!

Since children's health is extremely important for future growth and development great discretion is advised while giving antibiotics to children.

See also: KNOW WHAT PAINKILLERS TO TAKE.

Bet on Beta-Carotene

Study after study indicates that foods rich in beta-carotene and its other carotenoid brethren — for example, naturally occurring lutein and lycopene — are rich sources of antioxidants and help body's cancer-fighting systems reach their maximum efficiency.

The antioxidant plant pigment beta-carotene is also known as 'provitamin A' because it is converted into vitamin A (retinol and other forms) in the liver. It is found in whole milk, butter, cheese, egg yolk, liver, yellow and green vegetables like spinach, bell peppers and tomatoes and in fish. The same foods also contain a number of different carotene-like substances (carotenoids) that cannot be converted to vitamin A and so are wasted.

How much beta-carotene do you need?

A normal, well-balanced diet will provide quite enough retinol to prevent any such effects. If taken as a dietary supplement, 1 mg per day is equivalent to the recommended daily allowance and this dose is probably double the amount needed to prevent deficiency.

Although more research is necessary to answer that question, most scientists seem to feel that a normal, well-balanced diet will provide quite enough retinol. Foods that are rich in beta-carotene include papaya, spinach, broccoli, pumpkin, apricots, green pepper, mangoes and watercress. In general, dark green, orange and yellow fruits and vegetables are good sources of this vital nutrient.

Remember that vitamin A or its provitamin, beta-carotene, is not in the same safe category as vitamins C and E. No one knowledgeable would ever think of recommending mega-doses of vitamin A.

When Stomach Disagrees

A stomach ache is one of the more annoying things in life especially when you have things to do.

Reach for a light snack. When your stomach is hurting and you haven't been eating; having a snack is often the quickest way to ease the pain. Food in your stomach will absorb excess stomach acid, which can cause stomach aches. Good snacks include toasted wheat bread with a little honey or yogurt or some unsalted crackers.

Try steamed vegetables, mashed potatoes or clear vegetable soup. Bland snacks are best. This isn't the time to be eating spicy, chili or acidic foods like citrus fruits or tomatoes. And be sure to limit any acid filled drinks such as coffee, soda etc.

You can also opt for a herbal remedy. Herbal teas made from chamomile catnip, or *saunf* have been used for centuries for soothing digestive complaints, and many doctors believe they really are very helpful.

Activated charcoal which is used to cure flatulence can help relieve stomach aches by quickly absorbing excessive stomach acid.

Stomach ache is different from stomach pain. Stomach ache occurs commonly due to indigestion, acidity, menstrual cramps etc. Most of the time, a stomach ache shouldn't cause alarm. But if the ache persists or there is an acute pain then always consult a doctor.

See also: STOP BELLYACHING; DIARRHOEA: NATURE IS THE ANSWER; HOW MANY KINDS OF PAIN; DO BACTERIA IN YOUR DIGESTIVE TRACT HURT YOU.

Spinal Flexibility Test: It's Easy

The spinal flexibility test consists of bending over forwards while keeping your knees straight. At any age you should be able to touch the ground with your fingers. If you can't, and most of us can't, your spine has lost its youthful elasticity.

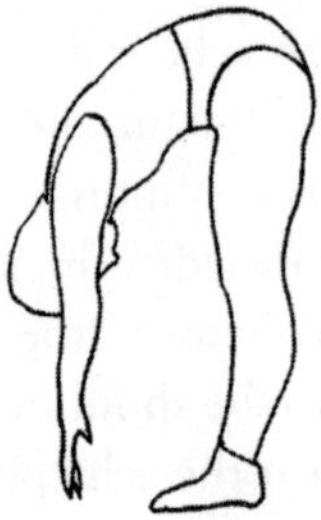

The loss of spinal flexibility eventually causes the vertebrae to impinge on the spinal nerves. Since the nerves from the spine go to all the organs and glands in the body, this results in an interference to the nerve supply to the organs and glands. This impairs their function, and we call this *functional* disease.

At this stage, the condition is reversible by skilful chiropractic manipulation of the spine and by yoga *asanas* (postures) to help regain and maintain the spine's flexibility.

Regularly performing stretching exercises for your back can help improve spinal flexibility and reduce the chances of injury and back pain, according to the US National Institute of Health (NIH). Flexibility exercises performed thrice a week and lasting at least 20 minutes can significantly improve back flexibility, say NIH experts.

See also: LIFTING PROPERLY; MINIMIZING EARLY MORNING BACKACHE.

Give Yourself a Helping Hand

Carpal tunnel syndrome is affecting increasing numbers of people who perform repetitive work with their hands. Computer operators, assembly line workers and musicians are at particular risk.

You can prevent carpal tunnel syndrome by minimizing the stress on your wrists and fingers. Take frequent breaks from any repetitive task, and perform hand exercises to relax the muscles and improve circulation.

Try massaging the front and back of your right hand with the thumb and fingers of your left hand. Gently massage the palm of your hand with your thumb and the back of your hand with your fingers. Now use your right hand to massage your left.

Another stress-buster involves grasping the four fingers of one hand with the other and gently bending your hand back at the wrist, holding them in that position for about five seconds.

Making a tight fist and then opening and closing your hand a number of times also relieves hand tension.

Finally, the easiest solution is to allow the hands to de-stress by not using the hands. Remember, numerous inter-connected muscles make-up your hand, and these muscles when used repetitively get tired. Be sure to give your hands a break every few hours to relieve stiffness and relax the hand muscles.

See also: TAILOR YOUR CHAIR, TAILOR YOUR DESK; TENSE YOUR MUSCLE TO RELAX.

Fats: The Good and the Bad

Not all fats are the same. There are different kinds of fat in the food you eat and some are better for you than others.

Monounsaturated fat. This type of fat is found in olive, canola and nut oils, as well as in nuts and avocados. Monounsaturated fat is considered a 'good' fat. It helps lower blood cholesterol, and it's more resistant to oxidation — a process that promotes the buildup of fat and cholesterol deposits in the arteries. However, because all fat — even monounsaturated fat — is high in calories, you should limit it to how much you eat.

Polyunsaturated fat. It is found in vegetable oils such as safflower, corn, sunflower, soy and cottonseed. It helps to lower 'bad' blood cholesterol, but it also lowers 'good' blood cholesterol, and is susceptible to oxidation.

Saturated fat. Saturated fats are animal fats such as those in red meat, dairy products and coconut and palm oils. These are 'bad' fats and tend to raise your blood cholesterol and increase risk of cardiovascular disease.

Trans fat. This type of fat is found in margarine that stays firm at room temperature, shortening and processed products made from them, such as pastry and other baked goods, crackers, candy and other snack foods. Trans fat — short for trans-fatty acids — raises blood cholesterol, and it may lower 'good' cholesterol, increasing cardiovascular disease risk. If you use margarine, look for products labelled as trans fat-free or that are made from canola oil.

See also: THERAPEUTIC OIL OF GODS; SLASH THE FAT; ADOPT AN ESKIMO DIET; KNOW YOUR CHOLESTEROL.

Why Practice Make Perfect?

When you repeat something — a musical note at the sitar, a tennis stroke, a list of foreign words — it is as if the repetition etches a groove in your brain. Don't take the analogy literally; there's no real groove in the brain. But repetition seems to cause anatomical and chemical changes that fix learned material in your memory and give you easy access to it.

No one is sure what those changes are. It is possible that parts of the neurons where memories are stored grow in size or number. There is also evidence that repeated stimulation of the neurons increases their output of memory-enhancing proteins. And there are indications that these and other changes strengthen the connections between neurons and facilitate the transmission of impulses along certain nerve pathways.

One important point to remember: practice makes for perfect performance only if what you practice is really what you want to remember. If you keep playing one wrong note in the music, if you keep pronouncing foreign words incorrectly, you will learn your mistakes, and you will find it very difficult to unlearn them subsequently.

So be sure you have it right (whatever 'it' might be) before you begin repeating it over and over to engrave it on your brain.

Why do the Elderly Remember the Past but not the Present?

Reminiscing at the age of 91, an actor complained that he had no idea what he had done five weeks before. Yet he hadn't forgotten the role he had played in a movie six decades ago. He could still deliver the memorable movie dialogues, though he had 'never looked at it from that day to this.'

Several factors contribute to that pattern in the elderly. The ability to acquire new memories often declines in old age, partly because of physical and chemical changes in the brain, partly because, with advancing years, preoccupations change and interest in the present may fall off. The brain tends to be less agile and numerous cognitive deficits may interfere in the neurological processes. At the same time, long-ago memories may sharpen with time, because they have had years to consolidate, that is, to leave indelible memory imprints in the brain. This may be especially true if they have been recalled repeatedly over the years because of their special emotional significance.

Confusion, disorientation and drowsiness — common symptoms of low sodium level may masquerade as the symptoms of other neurological conditions such as dementia, or memory loss, in the elderly. On-going confusion and low energy levels may be sign that you have chronically low sodium. Monitoring your fluid intake and your cognitive status are important aspects of care of the elderly.

See also: BALANCE YOUR SALT; BE FLEXIBLE AND LIVE TO BE 100.

Learn the Warning Signs of Diabetes

Most of us think of diabetes as a disease caused by eating a lot of sugar. Nothing could be farther from the truth. In fact, diabetes is a grave condition which affects the composition of our blood, the very element of life.

Diabetes is the condition where the body's ability to regulate the amount of glucose in the body is seriously impaired. The basic composition of the blood is altered and this affects almost every aspect of our health and life. It cannot be stressed enough that you should look out for the early warning signs of this life-altering condition. The sooner you recognize diabetes, the sooner you can get it treated.

Abnormal thirst, frequent urination, unusual hunger, rapid loss of weight, drowsiness, itching, a family history of diabetes, blurred vision, excessive weight, tingling, numbness or pain in the extremities, easy fatigue, skin infection or slow healing cuts, especially on the feet are signs of this condition.

There are two kinds of diabetes. The more severe form is known as Type I, which usually occurs before age forty and is treated with insulin injections. Type II diabetes usually begins after age forty. People who are overweight are at risk. Frequently, diet and exercise alone can control this form of the disease.

If you have any or some of these symptoms, make an appointment with your doctor. A simple blood test will reveal whether or not you have diabetes or even leading towards high blood glucose levels.

See also: LEARN CANCER'S WARNING SIGNS.

Quick Fixers or Stress Enhancers

People often turn to quick fixes to relieve their stress. These can produce a short, temporary relief, but they usually increase stress level in the long run.

Coffee and cigarettes are commonly used to relieve stress. The caffeine in coffee and the nicotine in cigarettes both stimulate the body's neuroendocrine system. This is also what stress does. The result is increased blood pressure, pulse rate and anxiety. The initial pleasant stimulation experience is at the expense of using up the body's energy reserves.

Alcohol, tranquillisers and sleeping pills have the opposite effects of coffee and cigarettes. They depress the body's neuroendocrine system. Initially they do relieve stress, but over a long period they will cause increased anxiety and depression. Tolerance can develop to these drugs and they can become addictive.

Coffee and alcohol in strict moderation will cause no harm, but keep away from cigarettes, tranquillisers and sleeping pills. If you are taking tranquillisers or sleeping pills, gradually reduce the dosage with the co-operation of your doctor.

Keep in mind that all the above will reduce the quality of your sleep, so your body will be less able to cope with stress, thus defeating the very purpose of the drugs. If you drink alcohol, drink just before your evening meal, since the food in your stomach will reduce the effect of the alcohol on your sleep.

See also: CUT DOWN CAFFEINE; SMOKING: ITS NEVER TOO LATE TO STOP.

Balance your Salt

Salt (sodium chloride) is an essential mineral our body needs to operate effectively. Sodium conducts electricity and regulates the amount of water around the body cells, but it is not a food.

Contrary to popular opinion, it's not necessary to include salt in your diet. It cannot be digested or assimilated by the body and has no nutritional value. The body's salt requirements are very low and are satisfied by the salt in natural foods, especially vegetables.

Salt is a major cause of high blood pressure, can cause incomplete digestion of protein foods by inhibiting the secretion of a protein-digestion enzyme called pepsin and lead to irritability of the nervous system.

To reduce salt intake, minimise adding salt to your food and reduce the intake of processed foods; they contain excess of salt. Check the labels on packaged food for their salt content before buying.

It is easy to make food taste good without using salt. Using herbs, spices and natural flavourings can help in enhancing taste of food. Some good options include bay leaf, dry mustard, nutmeg, onion, pepper, sage, thyme, ginger, oregano, parsley, curry powder, and lemon juice amongst many others.

Since salt deadens the taste buds, by reducing the salt intake you'll find that your taste buds will eventually enjoy the natural subtle flavours of food without salt.

However, reducing sodium too much can be just as harmful as consuming large amounts of it. Sodium deficiency can cause dehydration, heart palpitations, fatigue, restlessness, irritability, confusion, unconsciousness and even coma especially in the elderly.

Minimising Early Morning Backache

Do not be surprised if your back is stiff and achy in the morning. Joints tend to grow stiff when they are idle, as they are at night. Once you have had a chance to limber up, take a shower or make your cup of tea, the stiffness goes, and the back becomes more comfortable. This period of early morning stiffness is critical for back-pain suffers. Many spines are strained in the first 15 minutes of the day when rolling out of the bed, putting on socks or bending over the washbasin.

Before getting out of bed perform two simple exercises to stretch your spine and prevent backache.

One, lie on your back, clasp your hands round your knees and pull your knees firmly towards your chest.

Two, repeat this movement six times, then stretch your legs straight out in front and push first your left foot and then your right as far as possible down the bed.

Three, do this stretching movement six times with each leg; this will gently 'toggle' your pelvis from side to side and loosen the joints at the base of your spine.

You also need to develop a routine for getting out of bed which minimises the torsion at the base of your spine. Turn on your side with knees bent, as shown in figure on the facing page, then, in one smooth movement, drop your legs over the side of the bed so that you can use their weight to lever yourself into a sitting position, assisted by a gentle push from your elbows and hands. Do this while keeping the lower part of your spine as rigid as possible.

Once on your feet, carry out some gentle movements to stretch your spine. Animals perform these loosening exercises instinctively the moment they wake to overcome their post-inertial dyskinesia (disequilibrium on moving). We should follow their example and ape the early-morning stretching movements of a cat.

As far as possible, avoid heavy lifting and prolonged stooping during the first 15 minutes of each day. If you have to make your bed during this period, do so while kneeling on the floor rather than when bending from the waist. (If mattresses have to be turned, schedule this chore for midday on a weekend, rather than first thing on a weekday when you are likely to be stiff, tense and pressed for time.)

A

B

C

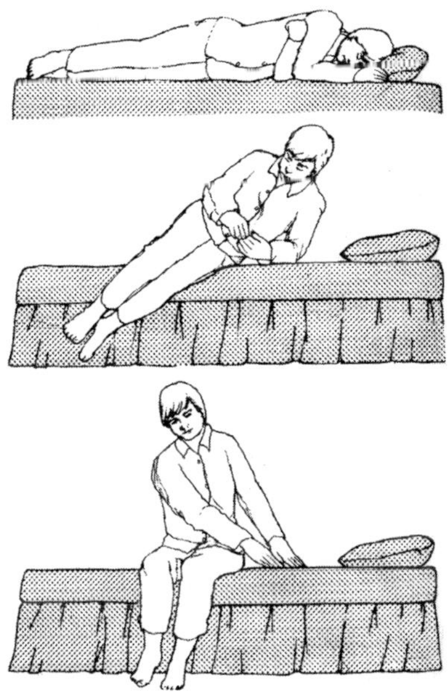

Getting out of bed: a) starting position, b) keep the spine straight and use the weight of the legs to raise the trunk, c) use a gentle push of the hands to get into a sitting position.

The Body's Thermostat

In spite of all external temperature changes experienced in an average day, most people maintain a fairly consistent internal body temperature of about 98.6°F (37°C), the temperature at which body processes work best. This miracle is accomplished with the help of a biological thermostat in the brain.

Near the base of the brain, is a structure called the hypothalamus whose main function is homeostasis, or maintaining body's status quo by governing the many autonomic (automatic or subconscious) systems of the body, including body temperature, blood pressure, fluid and electrolyte balance and body weight. It is often called 'brain of the brain'. By monitoring the temperature of the blood flowing through the body it triggers changes in the diameter of blood vessels. Suppose that the internal temperature rises above normal, which can happen if the weather or room temperature is very hot, if a person is exercising hard or has a fever, or simply because digestion and other normal body processes are producing a lot of heat. In that case, blood vessels to the skin expand or dilate. The volume of blood moving through them increases and carries the heat to the surface, where it dissipates. If, on the other hand, the internal temperature falls, the skin blood vessels will shrink or constrict, reducing blood flow to the surface of the body and thus conserving heat.

Doctors use a similar principle in some surgical operations on the heart or on the blood vessels. They frequently lower the patient's body temperature artificially to reduce the need for circulating blood through the body's organs while surgery is in progress.

A Diet for Good Vision

The eye is the only part of the human body that can function at 100 per cent ability at any moment, day or night, without rest. The eyelids need rest, but the eyes don't!

Everybody's heard of the old belief that eating carrots can help you see in the dark. That may or may not be true, but a rapidly growing body of evidence indicates that eating certain foods can indeed help to safeguard your vision and conversely certain foods can increase the risk of vision deterioration.

The most important nutrients essential to eye health are vitamins A, C and E, the anti-oxidants lutein and zeaxantin, some essential fatty acids and microelement zinc. An adequate intake of these nutrients lowers the risk of eye disease, maintain acuity of vision, protect the eye-tissue cells from damage by free radicals and ensure the proper function of the eye.

Vitamin A is found in egg yolk, wholemilk, turnip greens, drumsticks, beets, carrots, spinach, mangoes, apricots, raspberries; vitamin C in Indian gooseberries *(amla)* guava, limes, oranges, papayas, potatoes; vitamin E in vegetable oils, eggs, butter; zinc in cereals, nuts and oilseeds and copper in barley, walnuts, cashewnuts, whole lentils; all these are important for the eyes.

Generally speaking there are no foods bad for eyesight. A 2006 study by the Jean Meyer US Department of Agriculture (USDA) Human Nutrition Research Centre on Ageing found that certain high glycemic food like quickly digestable carbohydrates, candies etc. over a long period of time can damage the eye

The Magic of Sprouts

Sprouts are a powerhouse of nutrition. Sprouted grains are far more nutritious than unsprouted grains. They have low acid-forming properties and instead produce a beneficial alkaline state in the body.

Of all foods, sprouts are the richest source of vitamins, minerals and enzymes. By a process of natural transmutation, they have much greater nutrient content than the original food, as well as are easier to digest. For example, when oats are sprouted, the vitamin B content increases by 1000 per cent. When wheat is sprouted, the total vitamin content increases by 300 per cent. Similarly when *mung* beans are sprouted, the vitamin B content increases by up to 500 per cent and the vitamin A content by 200 per cent.

Being rich in vitamins and mineral, sprouts should constitute a substantial portion of a meal. They are a natural source of fibre which keeps the digestion system healthy, and helps you feel fuller between meals.

Sprouts contain healthy fats the essential fatty acids (EFAs) the body needs to perform basic body functions. A certain level of fat is needed to ward off infections and strengthen the immune system.

As sprouts are a 'living' food, they contain molecules of oxygen which are essential for healthy cells. Oxygen rich foods can ward off viruses and even kill bacteria.

From a nutritional and taste point of view, the best sprouts to eat, are alfalfa, *mung* beans, mixed beans, soybean, chickpeas (white and brown).

Sprouts contain a significant amount of vegetable proteins. They can even be a healthy alternative to meat, so if you are a vegetarian sprouts should be a part of your daily or weekly diet.

Personality Types: A and B

Based of extensive research, Dr Meyer Friedman and Dr Ray H. Rosenman, two American cardiologists who opened up the mind-heart connection, developed a model to define and categorise the behaviour style of people. Two personality types were defined by them — type A and type B personalities. The two types refer to specific patterns of behaviour rather than the overall personality of an individual.

Type A individual is defined as a person who is aggressively involved in incessant struggle to achieve more and more in less and less time, and if required, against the opposing efforts of other things or other persons. Such individuals tend to be strict, rigid, and perfectionists with an insatiable desire to achieve their goals, strong willingness to compete, strong desire for recognition and a desire to multitask under time constraints.

Type B individuals are perfect contrast to type A personalities. They are generally patient, easy-going, at times lacking urgency and are more relaxed in their approach to life. They tend to be more creative, imaginative and their actions and habits are inclined to self-analyse.

From their studies Drs Friedman and Rosenman concluded that men with type A behaviour pattern were twice as likely to suffer from heart disease than their more easy-going type B counterparts. 'How you react to your environment plays perhaps a far more important part in bringing on a heart attacks than what you eat, inhale or exercise,' declared Dr Friedman.

The Meyer Friedman Institute at San Francisco's Mount Zion Medical Centre is so named in recognition of his work.

Be Flexible and Live to be 100

The normal life span today is between sixty five and seventy five years. This does not imply that this is our *natural* life span.

The 'normal' life span is a life lived at variance to nature's laws. We overeat, eat too much of the wrong foods, under exercise, live stressful lives, sleep badly, breathe polluted air, and so on. This produces a life span far short of our true potential.

'Natural life span' is how long we would live if we lived how nature intended us to. There are two ways of assessing our natural life span:

1. Study people who live in more natural conditions, such as the Hunza people of northern Pakistan. The average life span of these people is around 100 years.
2. Study the ratio of life span to maturity age in animals who live in their natural, wild state. In this state most animals live seven times their puberty age. Relating this to humans, we arrive at around ninety years.

This means that we are dying about twenty plus years before we should. Not only that, but the last decade of life is often spent in a poor state of health, preventing us from fully enjoying our hard-earned retirement years.

Researchers have found that people who live to be 100 seem to have a number of personality traits in common. And all of these traits can be described by one word: flexibility.

Individuals who reach the century mark respond creatively to change, control their anxiety, integrate new ideas into their lives, and remain flexible and adaptable. And maybe most importantly, people who make it to 100 years of age really want to get there.

Intelligence: Nature or Nurture

Most psychologists today think of intelligence as a group of related abilities, including reasoning ability, creativity, insight, perseverance, flexibility, and the speed with which the brain processes information.

Majority of the intelligence tests in use reflect this view of intelligence as something multifaceted. Some tests measure just three components of intelligence: verbal, numerical, and reasoning abilities. Others measure such factors as memory span, verbal fluency, spatial perception, and the ability to classify, generalize, and reason by analogy.

After the age of seven or so, a person's IQ tends to stay about the same for the rest of his life. There are exceptions. Some studies show significant changes attributable at least partly to motivation and emotional factors.

Scientifically sound studies of directed efforts to raise IQ are limited, and the question of whether or not such efforts can succeed is much debated because of the nature or nurture aspect of intelligence. One scientist who did not believe that IQ is fixed was the leading American evolutionary biologist Stephen Jay Gould. 'We know,' he said, 'that "heritable" does not mean "inevitable." Genes do not make specific bits and pieces of a body; they code for a range of forms under an array of environmental conditions. Moreover, even when a trait has been built and set, environmental intervention may still modify inherited defects.'

So in short, while there is strong evidence that intelligence is 'inheritable' there is also supporting evidence that environment can and does affect our intelligence. Striking the 'right' balance is the key to a higher IQ.

Do the Bacteria in Your Digestive Tract Hurt You?

Normally, a multitude of bacteria flourish in our gut — both the small and the large intestines. The metabolic functions performed by these bacteria are like those of an organ, leading some scientists to call gut bacteria a 'forgotten' organ.

In the small intestine, certain kinds of bacteria foster the breakdown of food molecules into chemical substances that the tissues can absorb. The bacteria that inhabit the small intestine also prevent any harmful organisms in the large intestine from entering the ileum, the end of the small intestine. In the large intestine, some bacteria supplement the diet by manufacturing vitamins.

In short, these tiny inhabitants of our gut, help us to digest food, aid nutrient absorption, produce key vitamins, prevent disease and much, much more.

On occasions, especially when you are travelling, alien bacteria invade the intestines and cause 'traveller's dysentery,' or in India the infamous 'Delhi belly.' Very often the bacteria that trigger such fun-spoiling illnesses are not inherently harmful. They may inhabit the bodies of people native to a particular place without causing trouble, while visitors get sick because their body is not used to them.

See also: DIARRHOEA: NATURE IS THE ANSWER; STOP BELLYACHING; WHEN STOMACH DISAGREES; BE NICE TO YOUR LIVER.

Is There a Right Way to Blow Your Nose?

Blowing your nose seems more like a natural activity than a skill that must be learned. But, in fact, if you apply too much pressure to your nose when you blow it, you can rupture an eardrum or possibly send harmful germs into your ears or into your sinus cavities.

The American Medical Association recommends the following method for safe blowing: Clear one nostril at a time by pressing lightly on one side while you blow out the other. Blow frequently if the nose is congested, before mucus has a chance to build up. Use a soft, disposable tissue, and discard it where no one else will come in contact with it. And daub a little petroleum jelly on the nostrils if they become chapped and irritated.

Very small children have difficulty learning to blow the nose properly. Until they master the approved technique, you can use a simple, inexpensive hand aspirator to draw excess mucus out of the nose.

You can also help the child with a congested nose (and yourself, for that matter) by setting up a humidifier or vaporizer to moisten room air and speed mucus clearance. This is especially important during dry winter weather. But follow the instructions for use to the letter. If humidifiers are not cleaned and sterilized regularly, they can breed and spread infectious microorganisms.

What are the Primary Tastes?

Although they combine to make a myriad of different flavours, there are believed to be only four primary tastes: salt, sweet, sour, and bitter. These come from the chemical compounds in foods (or in other substances that you may put in your mouth).

Various parts of the tongue have taste buds that are especially sensitive to one of the basic sensations. You taste salty and sweet mainly on the front of the tongue, sour on the sides, and bitter at the back. The middle of the tongue registers almost no taste. Curiously, at least to some people, a single substance may taste sweet when it enters the front of the mouth but taste bitter by the time it reached the back; one such substance is saccharin.

Of the four primary tastes, the one that is most easily distinguished is the bitter. Its unmistakable taste serves as a protective mechanism. Many deadly toxins taste bitter, and their unpleasantness usually makes a person spit them out before they can do any damage.

A Twitchy Eyelid

From time to time your eyelid may take on a life of its own, twitching at random. This involuntary quivering of the eyelid muscle usually lasts less than a minute, but it can drive you crazy and make you wonder if something's wrong with your eyes.

A twitch is usually harmless. You may be able to relieve the twitching by gently massaging the affected eyelid. The cause of the twitching is unknown, but the condition is often associated with fatigue, stress, lack of sleep and excessive consumption of alcohol and / or caffeine.

Rarely, eye twitching may be the earliest sign of a chronic movement disorder, especially if other facial spasms develop in addition to the eye twitching.

According to Mayo Clinic the eye twitch usually goes away on its own within a few days or a few weeks. Schedule an appointment with your doctor if the twitching doesn't go away within one to three weeks; if your eyelid completely closes with each twitch; if twitching happens in other parts of your face as well; or your eye is red, swollen or has discharge, or you notice drooping eyelids.

Prevention is best when it comes to twitching. All in all you should work to relieve your stress and get as much rest as possible. If eye strain results in twitching, be sure you get plenty of breaks during the day to help rest your eyes and reduce the severity of your symptoms.

See also: AVOIDING CONJUNCTIVITIS; DRY EYES AND WATERY EYES.

What Are the Main Blood Types?

The differences in human blood are due to the presence or absence of certain protein molecules called antigens[1] and antibodies. The antigens are located on the surface of the red blood cells and antibodies are in the blood plasma. Individuals have different types and combinations of those molecules. The blood type you belong to depends on what you inherited from your parents.

It was the pioneering work of Austrian scientist Karl Landsteiner which made it possible to determine blood types; for his discovery he was awarded the Nobel Prize in Physiology/Medicine in 1930.

Blood has been classified into four types: A, B, AB, and O based on the ABO grouping system.

If your blood type is A, your red blood cells carry a protein called antigen A and your plasma, a protein called antibody B.

If you are type B, your blood contains antigen B and plasma carries antibody A. Blood type AB carries both antigens but no antibody, while type O blood has neither of the antigens but both of the antibodies.

These categories are important in blood transfusion because certain antigens and antibodies are hostile to each other, and can cause fatal blood-vessel blockages.

Generally, people with type A blood can safely receive blood from blood group A's and O's, while type B recipients are safe with blood from B's and O's.

People whose blood is type AB are known as universal recipients; their blood is compatible with types AB, A, B, and O. Type O people, on the other hand, are called universal donors; they can give blood to anyone.

[1] An antigen is a substance that stimulates the body to produce an antibody.

Are Nutritional Advantages the only Reason for Breastfeeding?

If one were to write down everything the mother and the baby gain from breast feeding, it would be a persuasive list. The prime consideration is the nutritional excellence of breast milk: its special suitability for babies during their first 6 to 12 months. Breastfeeding is the best form of nutrition for a newborn baby. Breast milk is nature's perfect food, meeting 100 per cent of a healthy infant's nutritional requirements, (with the possible exception of vitamin D) until a baby is six months old.

Almost all experts recommend breast milk rather than formula, not only because milk is highly nutritious, but also because it offers immunity against many childhood and adult diseases. The list of benefits to the infant by breastfeeding includes protection against gastrointestinal illness, diabetes, high blood pressure, heart disease and some cancers; prevention of allergies, obesity, respiratory illness; and improved blood pressure, bone health, cognitive function and iron status. Breastfeeding may also reduce anxiety later in childhood.

Perhaps one of the most important benefits for mothers is the immediate attachment that occurs with her baby during breastfeeding. The psychological benefit of this close bonding builds a trusting relationship. A mother may also experience an improvement in her self-esteem, derived from the assurance of knowing she is providing the best possible nutrition for her baby.

Less significant — but worth noting — are the practical advantages: no need to prepare formula or to worry about sterilizing bottles to ensure purity, and, of course, breastfeeding does not cost anything.

Use a Good Toothbrush and Use it Well

A toothbrush may seem like an easy purchase, but do spend time to make sure that your toothbrush is right for you.

For most of us, a soft-bristled toothbrush is the most comfortable and safest choice. Depending on how vigorously the teeth are brushed, medium- and hard-bristled brushes could actually damage the gums, root surface, and protective tooth enamel. Soft bristles are more flexible, and do not damage the gums. For greater protection, be sure the bristles on the toothbrush have rounded tips.

The best toothbrush head should allow easy access to all surfaces of your teeth. For most adults, a toothbrush head about 1.25 cm wide and 2.5 cm tall will be the easiest and the most effective to use. This makes it easier to clean certain hard-to-reach areas, such as the sides and backs of the molars.

A toothbrush should be replaced every three months or when bristles start to wear, which ever comes first. It is a good idea to buy two toothbrushes and use them in rotation. This allows each brush to dry thoroughly. After a cold, flu, sore throat or mouth infection do not overlook to replace your toothbrush with a new one. Germs can continue to live in the brush, and you can reinfect yourself.

A recent study revealed that the average person spends thirty seconds brushing his or her teeth instead of the recommended three to four minutes (although the people in the study estimated that they took more time brushing).

Observe your dental hygiene habits, and if you have any questions, do find time to talk to your dentist.

See also: BAD BREATH: HERE'S HOW TO MAKE IT FRESH; TOOTH DECAY AND TOOTH ACHES.

Fasting: The Greatest Remedy

Fasting is the oldest form of natural correction of physical imbalances; techniques can range from removal or reduction of one food substance to total abstention from all foods and liquids. Fasts may cover periods from a day or part of a day to more; there are recorded instances of persons going without food for periods in excess of sixty days.

The idea of fasting is based upon the principle that the stomach is the home of disease.

The logic of fasting is that it stops or greatly reduces the amount of food let into the digestive system, providing time for the body to clear itself of unprocessed foods, superfluities, and harmful pathogens. For some, it could be accomplished merely by eliminating meats or sugars from the diet, while for others, it may require total abstinence for some time.

Fasting is a purifying process which brings about a rapid elimination of toxic elements from the body. It corrects conditions of disordered nutrition and assimilation, and increases the activity of the eliminative organs, thus helping restore the entire system to health.

Almost all forms of therapeutic diets are varieties of fasting. The experiences of millions of persons who have used the fast to correct every kind of condition and disease, often after they failed to respond to any other treatment, proves the value of this natural method of cure. Nonetheless, long fasts conducted without proper supervision have resulted in severe damage. In many cases, a long fast so weakens the heart and other organs that a recovery is impossible. Safe and scientific fasting, therefore, consists of short, controlled fasts, repeated if necessary at various intervals.

Know Your Cholesterol

Cholesterol is a naturally occurring, fat-like substance with a complex chemical formula, and is used to build cells and make hormones. Some amount of cholesterol is necessary for healthy and proper functioning of the body cells. For example, the presence of cholesterol is essential for the formation of sex hormones and metabolism of vitamin D in the body. In young children, cholesterol is required for the development of brain cells.

Cholesterol in the blood comes from two main sources:

1. The cholesterol ingested from outside, that is taken in the daily diet. An average vegetarian consumes between 200-400 mg of cholesterol daily, while a non-vegetarian usually consumes between 400-600 mg of cholesterol.
2. A large part of the cholesterol in the blood comes from the cholesterol production within the liver.

High blood cholesterol is recognised and accepted as a major risk factor in heart attacks and heart disease. It has been established that by reducing cholesterol level by one per cent, the risk of heart disease is reduced by two per cent.

The total blood cholesterol is the sum total of cholesterol carried by three kinds of lipoproteins: very low density lipoproteins (VLDL), low density lipoprotein (LDL) and high density lipoprotein (HDL).

HDL is often referred to as 'good cholesterol' and LDL as 'bad cholesterol'.

By far the most comprehensive and widely accepted standard of total blood cholesterol level is that of US National Cholesterol Education Programme:

< 200 mg = Desirable
200-239 mg = Borderline High
> 240 mg = High Risk

It has been noted that even if total cholesterol is well within the normal limit of 200 mg, a person may still have low level of HDL, the 'good cholesterol', which is associated with increased risk of heart disease.

You should consider yourself in high risk category if you are a male, above 45 years of age, have a family history of Coronary Heart Disease (CHD), are a cigarette smoker, have high blood pressure or diabetes and are overweight.

Now the good news. Heart disease due to high blood cholesterol is both avoidable and curable. In almost all cases high blood cholesterol can be controlled and reversed through changes in life style, diet and regular exercise; only a few require medication and surgery.

High fibre intake can reduce chances of CHD, diabetes and obesity. High intake of soluble fibre has been found to reduce cholesterol by 20 to 25 per cent. Fruit and vegetables are rich in fibre as well as in vitamins and minerals. Fish and fish oil are known to reduce the bad cholesterol. Foods which are strictly no-no are red meat, egg yolk, cheese and all types of saturated fats. Finally, it is important to exercise and keep your weight within the recommended range.

Despite all the current hoopla over cholesterol levels, the blood tests given to check your cholesterol levels leave a lot to be desired. Some problems are caused by the equipment used. The tabletop machines used in public screenings can give varying results, from 200 to 250 for the same sample. But even the most sophisticated equipment can be off by 5 per cent.

In order to get accurate reading you must do two things:

Fast for 8 to 12 hours before a test to measure your HDL and LDL components.

Always get a second test and compare levels.

Talk to your doctor about how often you should get your cholesterol checked.

See also: ADOPT AN ESKIMO DIET; FATS: GOOD AND BAD; SLASH THE FAT; THERAPEUTIC OIL OF THE GOODS.

Loveable Legumes

The term legume refers to a large family of plants, including beans, lentils and peas, whose seeds develop inside pods and are usually dried for ease of storage. They are among the most versatile and nutritious food available.

Legumes are low in fat contain no cholesterol but are high in fibre, protein, folate, potassium, iron, magnesium and phytochemicals. The fibre in legumes is mostly soluble, which may help lower cholesterol and help regulate blood sugar levels. In addition, legumes — which include soybeans, peanuts, lima beans, chickpeas, black-eyed peas, split peas and lentils — are versatile and inexpensive. They're a healthy substitute for meat, which has more fat and cholesterol. If you use canned legumes, rinse them well to eliminate salt that may have been added during processing.

As you add more beans and legumes to your diet, be sure to drink enough water and exercise regularly to help your gastrointestinal system handle the increase in dietary fibre.

See also: MAGIC OF SPROUTS; FEAST ON FIBRE; DRINK UP.

Put on Your Walking Shoes

Walking is the cheapest and possibly the healthiest form of exercise; this is one reason for its popularity. And its absolutely free — no expensive equipment, no special clothing; the only essential item is a pair of comfortable walking shoes.

A good walking shoe must support your foot where it needs support and provide flexibility where your foot bends.

When buying walking shoes, look for shoes with a rounded, roomy toe compartment. This will help prevent calluses on the tops and sides of your toes.

Inside the shoe look for a padded heel collar to reduce chafing; a padded tongue and ankle to protect the front of your foot and a smooth, absorbent lining. This will ensure protection and comfort.

To stabilize the foot through its forward roll and to keep it from rolling from side to side opt for shoes with heel counter. For more support, look for a heel counter that extends all around the side of the shoe toward the arch.

A rocker shape provides flexibility and proper heel strike. Choose a natural heel-to-toe curve. Heel should be slightly bevelled.

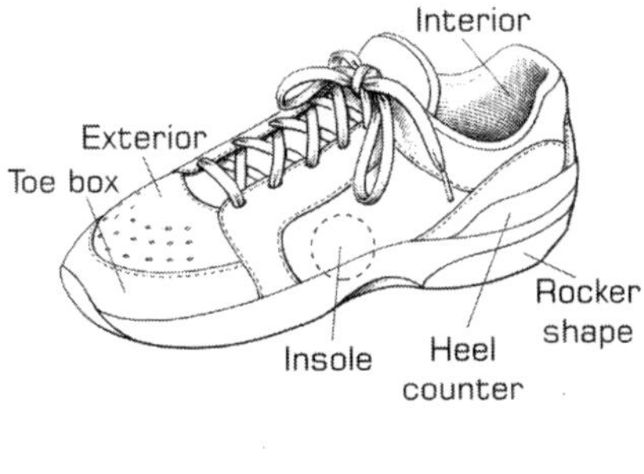

Shoes with removable insoles that you can air out or replace are always a more sensible choice.

Last but not the least, choosing shoes with uppers made of breathable materials will provide comfort and durability.

Aim for Your Target Heart Rate

Learn how to determine what your heart rate should be during aerobic exercise. Exercise physiologists have determined how long your heart has to beat at a certain rate for you to benefit from your exercise.

To get the most benefit from aerobic exercise, for example, your heart should stay within what is called your training zone. The training zone is a range which determines the high end and low end of the target heart rate. The American College of Sports Medicine and other fitness groups use a standard formula to determine what a person's training zone is:

Subtract your age from 220, multiply that number by 0.7 to find the low end of your training zone. Multiply it by 0.85 to find the high end of your training zone.

During exercise, take a moment to find your pulse. Using the second hand on your watch, count the number of pulses in one minute (or count your pulse in ten seconds and multiply by six). This is your heart rate. Compare your heart rate with your training zone. If you're at the beginning or end of your workout, your heart rate should be at the low end of your training zone. If you're at the height of your workout, it should be at the high end. If your heart rate is higher than your training zone, you're exercising too hard. If it's lower, you're not working hard enough to really benefit from the exercise.

Scientists discovered the maximum heart rate normally declines with age: a young child can elevate heart rate to in excess of 200 beats per minute, whereas a 60-year-old peaks around 160 beats per minute.

See also: AEROBIC VS ANAEROBIC EXERCISE; GET UP AND GET GOING.

Try a Water Workout

A walk or a workout in water can do wonders for your health! Water walking and exercising was first developed to help people with injuries exercise. But it wasn't long before experts in rehabilitative therapy saw that this exercise could be of benefit to everyone.

Exercising in water cushions and protects the body against impact injuries which may result from exercising on hard surface.

Do each move for two minutes in the pool's shallow end:

1. *Jog in place.* Keep knees high.
2. *Tick-tock hop.* Quickly jump from side to side, keeping feet together.
3. *Knee twist.* Cross right elbow toward left knee at waist. Alternate sides.
4. *Bicycle.* Lean with back against side of pool, arms outstretched at edge. 'Pedal' legs at surface.
5. *Outer-thigh lift.* Stand with left side near wall, feet together, holding edge with left hand. Lift right leg out to side. Do 20 reps on each side.
6. *Flutter kick.* Hold onto edge of pool, arms extended; kick legs quickly.
7. *Crunch.* From bicycle, extend legs, keeping feet together. Pull both knees into chest. Return to starting position.

If you workout in water, check the temperature to make sure the water is in the comfort zone of between 82° and 86°F.

If you water-walk at a steady pace, you can burn off 300 to 500 calories an hour. And because you have to overcome the water's resistance, water walking at comfortable speed of three kilometers an hour gives you the same benefit as walking on land at four kilometers an hour. Of course, if you walk in shallow water, which has less resistance, you'll need to walk faster than in deeper water.

Understanding Food Poisoning

Food-borne illness, usually referred to as 'food poisoning' is a growing problem in most parts of the world and more so in Asia due to contaminated water supply, poor hygiene and careless food handling. The other reasons are increased travel and more outside-the-home dining. Cases of food poisoning are more evident in monsoons and summer months.

All foods contain small amounts of bacteria. But when food is poorly handled, improperly cooked or stored, bacteria can multiply in great enough numbers and cause illness.

If you become ill within 1 to 6 hours after consuming contaminated food or water, you probably have a common type of food poisoning. Symptoms include nausea, vomiting, diarrhoea or stomach pain.

Rest and drink plenty of liquids. Don't use antidiarrhoeal medications because they may slow elimination of the bacteria and toxins from your system.

Mild to moderate illness often resolves on its own within 12 hours. If the symptoms are severe or persist for more than 12 hours, it is recommended that you consult your doctor.

Food poisoning can cause various ailments but whether a person falls ill or not depends on the organism, the amount of exposure, and the state of health.

As we get older, our immunity system does not respond as quickly and effectively to infections as in the younger years. Conditions such as diabetes, cancer treatment can also reduce your immune response, making you more susceptible to food-borne illness.

See also: DIARRHOEA: NATURE IS THE ANSWER; HANDWASHING: THE WHY AND THE HOW; WHEN STOMACH DISAGREES; STOP BELLYACHING.

Cuts, Scratches and Wounds

Everyday cuts, scratches or wounds don't often require a trip to the doctor. Yet proper care is essential to avoid infection or subsequent complications.

Minor cuts and scratches usually stop bleeding on their own. If not, apply gentle pressure with a clean cloth or bandage to stop the blood.

It is important to keep the wound clean. Rinse the wound with clean water and clean the surrounding area of dirt with a wash cloth. If dirt is embedded in the wound after cleaning, don't attempt to remove it by yourself, instead a medically trained person should handle it. Cleaning the wound also reduces the risk of contracting tetanus. Puncture wounds or other deep cuts, animal bites or particularly dirty wounds carry risk of tetanus infection. A dirty or deep wound may need a booster dose if you have not had one in the previous one year.

After you clean the wound, apply a thin layer of an antibiotic cream or ointment (such as Neosporin or Polysporin) to help keep the surface moist. This will not only heal the wound faster, but will discourage infection and allow body's healing system to close the wound more efficiently. Be aware that ingredients in some ointments may cause a mild rash in some people. If rash appears, stop using the ointment.

Exposure to air will speed healing, but bandages help to keep the wound clean and keep harmful bacteria out. Draining blisters are vulnerable and should be covered until a scab forms.

To help prevent infection, change the dressing at least once a day or whenever it becomes wet or dirty.

See also: CLEAN OUT YOUR MEDICINE CABINET; TRAVEL WITH A MEDICINE KIT; KNOW WHAT PAINKILLERS TO TAKE.

Tooth Decay and Tooth Aches

In most people, whether children or adults, tooth decay or cavities, also called caries, is the main cause of toothaches. Tooth decay mainly is caused by bacteria which thrive on the sugar and carbohydrates in the food. These bacteria are present in a thin, almost invisible film on the teeth called plaque.

Tooth decay takes time to develop, often a year or two in permanent teeth but less in primary teeth. The decay-producing acid formation occurs within the first 20 minutes after you eat and attacks the plaque or the protective film on the outer surface of the teeth. They eat through the tooth enamel creating tiny cavities or openings in the tooth's surface.

The first sign of decay may be a sensation of pain when you eat something sweet, very cold or very hot. Until you are able to see your dentist you can try sucking on an ice cube placed in the area of irritation or using one of the several over-the-counter pain relievers. These will offer temporary relief. Application of oil of cloves is also helpful in relieving pain. It is available widely. The traditional Indian grandma's remedy for quick but temporary relief from tooth pain is to keep a whole clove (*laung*) on the affected tooth and suck on it.

Brushing and flossing help limit bacteria on your teeth and thus prevent tooth decay. Get into a routine for brushing regularly. At a minimum, the American Dental Association recommends that you brush your teeth twice a day; one time should be before sleep. But if you snack and drink throughout the day, it may be helpful to brush your teeth more often. Floss at least once a day. Flossing helps to remove any food particles wedged between the teeth.

Prevention is the best way to avoid tooth decay and cavities.

Happy Feet

Choosing footwear that properly fits your feet can prevent a multitude of foot problems. Wear shoes that address your specific foot needs. Everyone's feet are different.

In a survey by the American Podiatric Medical Association (APMA) 73 per cent women admitted to experience foot pain and discomfort as a result of their shoes.

Here are some tips to keep your tootsies happy and pain free.

1. Have your feet measured before you make a shoe purchase. Make sure you measure both feet, since most of us have one foot larger than the other. Always purchase shoes to fit the larger foot. There should be about 1.25 cm space between your longest toe and the end of the shoe.

   Feet tend to get larger as we grow older, have children and gain weight.

2. The ball of your foot should fit comfortably into the widest part of the shoe.
3. Your feet swell during the day, so make sure you only shop for shoes in the evening.

Before you purchase a pair of shoes grasp the shoe at the front and back, and bend it. If the shoe bends in the middle, it will probably not give the support you need. If the shoe bends at the ball of your foot, it will.

Try on several different pairs before taking the final decision. Put both shoes on and walk in them before you buy. Sizes vary, as do styles and shoe shapes.

Shoes have a considerable bearing on the posture and the back. High heeled shoes are injurious for the back. If you prefer shoes with laces, take care that the laces are tied properly. Untied laces make you curl your toes to grip the soles and that harms your back.

Don't Try to be a 'Super Mom'

A mother who works has two jobs: the first one begins when she gets everyone else off to work and school, and the second one starts when she arrives at her own job. When she gets home, her first job picks right up again.

If you're a working mother, you're probably working twice as hard as your husband, even if he helps out around the hours. And if you're working and raising your children alone, you have an even more difficult burden. Here are a few tips to keep both you and your kids happy, healthy and sane.

- Set aside some time to do something just for yourself.
- Organize household tasks efficiently. Delegate some responsibility for household chores to your kids.
- Schedule your tasks and stick to your schedule.
- Reward yourself every now and then for all the work that you do.
- A weekly family calendar of important dates helps avoid 'deadline panic'.
- Eliminate time-consuming misunderstandings by communicating clearly and listening carefully.
- Fight the guilt. Remember: Having a family and a job is normal — for both women and men. If nothing helps, tell your kids how you're feeling chances are they'll understand.

See also: LISTEN TO YOUR CHILDREN.

How Many Kinds of Pain are There?

Cramping, throbbing, nauseating, sharp: those are just a few of the words persons use to describe the kind of pain they were feeling. But physiologists generally speak of two kinds of pain. What they call 'first pain' is described as quick, sharp, and easy to localize: you know just where you hurt. 'Second pain,' is diffuse, nagging, particularly hard to bear and you may have a hard time telling just where it originates; nearly always, however, it comes from deep inside the body.

Pain is transmitted via the spinal cord to the thalamus inside the brain which makes us aware of the pain.

With a heat lamp used to raise the temperature of the skin gradually, most people first report sensations of pain when their skin reaches 113°F or 45°C. (The temperature at which heat begins to damage body tissues.) Practically everyone reports feeling pain before the temperature rises to 116.6°F or 47°C.

A person's pain threshold is the least intense stimulus (the least forceful blow, or prick) that feels painful. Studies suggest that most people have roughly the same pain threshold.

However, people have different reactions to pain. What maybe intolerable to one may not bother another, even though both feel pain. Tolerance for pain may vary with circumstances and psychological state, even in the same person. If you should stub your toe while running away from a fierce dog it probably wouldn't hurt at all. Hospitals report that preoperative psychological preparation seems to reduce post-operative pain. Patients who are told in advance how much pain to expect and for how long generally need fewer painkillers than do unprepared patients.

Add Years to Your Life at Lunchtime

Take a brisk walk for thirty minutes or so every day at lunchtime and add years to your life.

How?

A brisk walk burns almost as many calories as jogging. Plus, it raises your metabolism, tones your muscles and lifts your mood. The result is a healthier life.

A recent study by the Cooper Institute for Aerobics Research, Dallas, Texas, and founded by the 'father of aerobics' Dr Kenneth H Cooper, showed, for example, that moderate everyday activity such as walking provides significant protection from cardiovascular disease, cancer and a host of other disorders. The study was carried out over an eight-year period and involved more than 13,000 men and women.

So get away from your desk at lunchtime and take a walk. You'll be doing something good for your health, and you'll likely be more energized all afternoon!

See also: AEROBIC VS ANAEROBIC EXERCISES.

Are Males more Aggressive than Females?

The popular opinion holds as males being more aggressive than females. As proof they cite boys as being physically and verbally move aggressive than girls and the relative lack of women in the world's armed forces or even in physically aggressive and demanding sports like rugby, football and ice-hockey.

In addition, there is corroborative evidence from anthropology showing that killing — whether it be in war or in daily life — occurs in thousands of different cultures and that the people who do the killing are chiefly men. If a sex difference is universal among human beings even though they grow up in very different cultures, there is a good chance that the difference comes not from the way people are brought up but from biological factors that are presumably the same in every society.

But as to the question of whether or not aggressiveness is based largely on biology — on physiological differences between the sexes rather than on learning — some scientists consider the evidence now available to be inconclusive.

However, there are a number of scientists who are convinced that aggression can be traced to the male hormone testosterone. In one especially provocative study of male juvenile delinquents, the most aggressive ones were those with the highest levels of testosterone in their bodies.

But, finally remember, not all men are more aggressive than women; some women are more aggro than most men.

See also: PERSONALITY TYPES: A AND B.

The Pain of Male Menopause

If you're a male between ages forty and sixty, you may go through emotional changes that some experts call male menopause. You may begin to feel pessimistic, overburdened, nervous and dissatisfied. Or you may have trouble sleeping, begin to abuse alcohol and/or drugs, become unhappy at work and at home, and develop sexual problems. You suddenly may even consider taking big risks with your life.

So what is the best way to understand male menopause? Many doctors attribute it to lower testosterone levels due to ageing. Testosterone gradually decline throughout adult life — about one per cent every year after the age of 30 to 35 years.

If you think you're undergoing male menopause, stay away from the 'relief' offered by drugs and alcohol. Talk to your spouse and close friends. Sharing your feelings will ease the tension you feel. Don't make major changes impulsively, such as quitting your job. Step back. And think things over.

Eat a healthy diet and include physical activity as part of the daily routine. Healthy lifestyle helps maintain strength, energy and lean muscle mass. Regular physical activity also promotes better sleep and a 'feel good' factor.

If your problems persist, consider talking about it to a professional.

See also: MEN: ADD TOMATOES TO YOUR DIET; CHECK YOUR TESTICLES; TAKE IT EASY; CHERISH YOUR FRIENDS.

Sweating and Body Odour

Sweating or perspiration is natural and healthy. It is body's normal response to a build-up of body heat due to exercise or exertion, a warm environment or when a person is anxious or under stress.

Sweating varies widely from person to person. Drinking hot beverages, more so if they contain caffeine, and alcohol may trigger a light sweating in some. Others simply inherit a tendency to sweat heavily.

For most, sweating is an uncomfortable nuisance. Body odour is more troublesome. Although sweat is practically odourless, it tends to take on an unpleasant odour when it comes into contact with bacteria on the skin.

Odour usually is more likely to develop at places which are not exposed to air and therefore damp, such as armpits and feet in socks and shoes. Regular bathing and wearing clothes made of natural fibre allow the skin to breathe which helps keep the amount of bacteria on the skin in check. In tropical climates select cotton or silk fabrics; while exercising or playing sport wear fabrics that can wick moisture away from your skin.

Microorganisms thrive in the damp spaces between your toes. Dry your feet thoroughly before getting into socks and shoes. Wear cotton socks that absorb moisture and shoes made of natural materials, such as leather or fabric, which allow air circulation and help keep the feet dry. It is recommended that you rotate your shoes and not wear the same pair two days in a row if you have sweaty feet. Shoes may not completely dry over-night, especially during the rainy season or in damp regions.

Finally, air your feet. Go barefoot when you can, or at least slip out of your shoes now and then.

Listen to Your Children

Most people can remember some hard times from their youth, but today there are even more sources of stress for even younger children: increasing number of marriages end in divorce; both parents often work; alcohol, drugs and cigarettes are more readily available, and the pressure from peers to engage in sexual activity is significant.

Besides creating unhappy children, stressful conditions can result in physical illness or emotional problems. One of the most important things you can do to prevent this is to encourage a child to express his or her feelings. Communicate with your child from the earliest years on, and you can not only prevent many problems but also greatly minimize those that do occur.

Spend quality time with your children and become a good role model. Play with them. Take them outdoors. Read to them and with them. Share a joke. Encourage them to participate in physical activities at school and in the neighbourhood. All these will go a long way in keeping the communication open and keep the 'generation gap' away.

See also: TREAT YOUR CHILDREN WELL; GO WHERE YOU'RE NEVER GONE BEFORE.

The Good, the Bad and the Bonus

Five Good Habits — Adopt them:

- Eat a healthy breakfast, but don't eat too much.
- Eat at least 3 to 4 servings of vegetables and fruits a day.
- Eat whole grains, such as whole-grain bread.
- Eat healthy fats, such as olive oil and nuts.
- Walk or exercise for at least 30 minutes a day.

Five Bad Habits — Eliminate them:

- Don't watch TV while eating, and spend no more time watching TV than you do exercising.
- Eat no sugar except what is naturally found in fruit.
- Eat no snacks except vegetables and fruits.
- Limit the amount of meat and low-fat dairy that you eat.
- Eat no restaurant food unless it fits in the diet program.

Five Bonus Habits — Add them:

- Keep record of what you eat.
- Keep record of your physical activity.
- Walk or exercise at least 60 minutes a day.
- Eat mostly fresh foods and healthy frozen or canned foods.
- Write down your daily goals.

A Peep into the Future: Six Life Altering Breakthroughs

It sounds like science fiction but astounding medical breakthroughs are likely in the next decade or so. Research is happening right now that will change the quality of our life, probably extend it and definitely make the lives of our children healthier and longer than we ever thought possible.

1. The Blind will See
Scientists have already tested and continue to research microchip implants to help people regain their sight. Scientists are working on deep brain implants, coupled with special glasses, that can bring sight to unsighted. In the next ten years, being blind will be a thing of the past.

2. Organs on Order
Tissue engineering or regenerative medicine allows scientists to grow new organs to replace diseased or damaged organs. Using tissue from the patient's own existing organ or synthetic materials, scientists are experimenting growing replacements in a laboratory. Engineered replacement organs would eliminate problems associated with donor organs and dramatically lower the costs.

3. Brain Repair
For someone who's had a stroke or suffers from Alzheimer's or other neurological diseases, the advancements in neural enhancements offer great hope. Using microchips or a matrix of fibre optic wires to bridge damaged areas of the brain appears to be a way to cure a number of neurological conditions. The use of microchips to bridge neural pathways also opens doors to the possible expansion of brain use for everyone.

4. Eradication of Genetic Conditions
With the completion of the human genome project[1], scientists know more than ever about the genetic structure and how it affects us. Researchers and scientists are using DNA based therapy to vaccinate people against fatal diseases; designer medicines are being experimented with which are disease or gene specific. We are already at the cusp of future where genetic conditions may no longer exist. It may even be possible to create 'designer' babies with higher intelligence, beauty and talent.

5. Hope for Heart Disease
It appears that stem cells can help prevent heart attacks by stimulating the growth of new blood vessels around the heart. The Food and Drug Administration of USA recently approved a study to test this in which scientists will take adult stem cells from the bone marrow of patients and inject them into their clogged arteries. The hope is that new vessels will grow and increase the blood flow to the heart.

6. The End of Cancer Deaths
Nanotechnologists already have developed treatments for certain types of cancer, and scientists are discovering more all of the time; tumours of less than one tenth of an inch can be detected and targeted without killing normal cells. Researchers are producing drugs that show early success at preventing tumour growth by cutting of its blood supply. Officials at the U S National Cancer Institute predict that in the next two decades or so all cancer deaths will be preventable.

~

As exciting these breakthroughs appear to be, yet there are ethical and practical issues involved that confront lawmakers, philosophers, sociologists, academicians and all thinking persons. How will the society change if we live 20 or 30 years longer? How far will we, or should we, go to create the 'perfect human being' — genetically engineered to be smart, beautiful, and disease-free; or consider the flip side, a perfect killing machine, a criminal genius?

How will these exciting technologies be exploited for greed and self-interest?

[1] Human Genome Project refers to 13-year international effort to identify estimated 20,000-25,000 human genes and make them accessible for further biological study.

Appendix 1

Determining Your Body Mass Index

Although the weight chart is generally very helpful, a better way to find out whether you are obese or not is to determine your Body Mass Index (BMI). BMI takes into account both your height and weight in determining whether there is excess fat. The BMI chart that is considered the 'measurement of choice' by many researchers who study obesity.

The BMI is an improvement over other weight/height tables because it is based on an individual's body mass rather than on a sample of people, but it still does not provide a measure of the fatness or leanness of the body. To do that, one's body-fat content must be assessed. The formula to calculate BMI is:

$$\text{BMI} = \frac{\text{Weight in kg}}{(\text{Height in metres})^2}$$

BMI Recommendations

Age Groups	Recommended BMI
18-34 years	17-28
35-54 years	17-29
> 55 years	17-30

BMI range as recommended/followed by Life Insurance Corporation of India.

Interpretation: BMI over the recommended range indicates overweight and cautions us to get back into the ideal range. Children and pregnant women have different BMI guidelines.

Appendix 2

Add Vitamins to Your Life

A balanced diet usually provides adequate amounts of vitamins, minerals and other nutrients. But sometimes it can't satisfy all your nutritional needs — such as when you're ill, pregnant or taking medication.

Vitamin supplements offer important nutrition and also have an important role in strengthening the body's immune system, preventing certain illnesses and slowing down the age related degeneration.

All vitamins come with the Daily Values on their labels. The amounts listed on the next page are for healthy adults averaging 2000 calories per day. Amounts vary for children, elderly, lactating/pregnant women or those with chronic diseases or those who consume less than 2000 calories per day. These are the recommendations of The Food and Nutrition Board of the American Institute of Medicine. The recommended dietary allowances (RDA) are the minimum amount required to avoid deficiency. (Some experts believe that these limits are too low). The Daily Value represents the amount you need to prevent a deficiency in that vitamin (and it may actually be much lower than the amount you need to take).

Vitamins	Main Sources	Daily Dose
Vitamin A (Retinol)	Liver, egg yolk, milk green and yellow vegetables and fruits	M: 1000 mcg W: 800 mcg
Vitamin B_1 (Thiamine)	Wholegrain cereals, legumes, lotus stems, Bengal gram, pineapples	M: 1.2-1.5 mg W: 1-1.2 mg
Vitamin B_2 (Riboflavin)	Green vegetables, yellow fruits like mangoes and papayas, liver, eggs	M: 1.3 mg W: 1.1 mg
Vitamin B_3 (Niacin)	Liver, meats prawns rice, wheat, sunflower seeds, green vegetables, almonds	M: 16 mg W: 14 mg
Vitamin B_5 (Pantothenic acid)	Yeast, liver, eggs, peanuts, mushrooms, soya beans	M: 5 mg W: 8 mg
Vitamin B_6 (Pyridoxine)	Yeast, sunflower seeds, wheat germ, lentils, bananas, walnuts	M: 1.3-1.7 mg W: 1.3-1.7 mg
Vitamin B_8 (Biotin)	Liver, rice bran, rice, peanut butter	M: 30 mcg W: 30 mcg
Vitamin B_9 (Folic acid)	Pulses & legumes, green vegetables	M: 400 mcg W: 400 mcg
Vitamin B_{12} (Cyanocobalamin)	Liver, meat, eggs, shrimps, milk	M: 2.4 mcg W: 2.4 mcg
Vitamin C (Ascorbic acid)	Citrus fruits & vegetables, Indian gooseberries, guavas, potatoes	M: 90 mg W: 75 mg
Vitamin D	Sunlight, fish liver oil	M: 5-10 mcg W: 5-10 mcg
Vitamin E (Tocopherol)	Cold-pressed crude vegetable oils eggs, butter, sprouted seeds and grains	M: 10 mg W: 8 mg
Vitamin K	Cauliflower, cabbage, spinach, alfalfa, oats, yogurt	M: 70-80 mcg W: 60-65 mcg.

Deficiency Symptoms
Inflammation of the eyes, poor vision, nightblindness, lack of appetite and vigour, defective teeth and gums, skin disorders (pimples, acne, boils) retarded growth in children, dry and dull hair, ridged nails.
Loss of appetite, poor digestion, chronic constipation, loss of weight, depression, insomnia, beriberi, nervous disorders
Vision defects (cataract), impaired growth, sore lips, dull/oily hair or skin, premature wrinkles
Coated tongue, sores in the mouth, anaemia irritability, nervousness, diarrhoea, insomnia, weakness of the nerves, depression, migraine, pellagra
Chronic fatigue, infections, greying/loss of hair, constipation, skin disorders, insomnia, retarded growth, painful and burning feet, low blood sugar, low blood pressure
Anaemia, oedema, mental depression, skin disorders, tooth decay, eczema, kidney stones, migraine, premature senility
Muscular weakness, pricking of the skin, lack of appetite, eczema, dandruff, hair loss, anaemia, lung infections, fatigue, depression
Anaemia in pregnant women and children, spontaneous abortions and difficult labour, impaired circulation, fatigue, skin pigmentation, anaemia
Anaemia, poor appetite and retarded growth in children, chronic fatigue, sore mouth, feeling of numbness or stiffness, loss of mental energy.
Scurvy, soft gums, skin haemorrhages, anaemia, slow healing of sores and wounds, premature ageing, thyroid insufficiency
Rickets, tooth decay, pyorrhoea, brittle or soft bones, retarded growth, premature ageing
Heart and lung disease, brain stroke, loss of sexual potency, abortions, miscarriages
Severe haemorrhages, blood taking longer to clot, nosebleeds

Appendix 3

The Healthy Eating Pyramid[1]

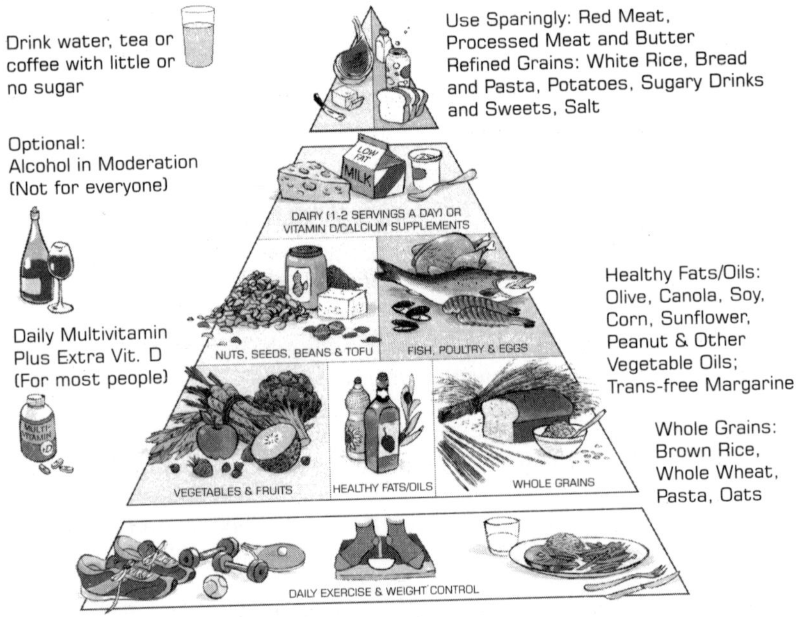

The Healthy Eating Pyramid is a simple, trustworthy guide to choosing a healthy diet. Its foundation is daily exercise and weight control, the two elements that strongly influence our health. It builds from there, showing that you should eat more foods from the bottom (vegetables, whole grains) and less from the top (red meat, refined grains, potatoes, sugary drinks, and salt).

The Healthy Eating Pyramid is not a rigid road map but a simple, general, flexible guide to what you should eat.

---

1 Developed by Walter C. Willett, MD and Patrick J. Skerrett, Harvard School of Public Health.

The other bricks of the Pyramid include the following, starting from the bottom:

Whole Grains: The body uses carbohydrates mainly for energy, and the best grain sources of carbohydrates are whole grains such as oatmeal, whole wheat bread, and brown rice. Since the body is unable to digest whole grains as quickly as it can highly processed carbohydrates such as white flour, these help to keep hunger at bay.

Healthy Fats and Oils: Healthy unsaturated fats include olive, canola, soy, corn, sunflower, peanut, and other vegetable oils; nuts, seeds, and avocados; and fatty fish such as salmon.

Vegetables and Fruits: The more veggies — and more the variety — the better. Potatoes don't count as a vegetable, since they have the same effect on blood sugar as refined grains and sweets. That's why potatoes are in the 'Use Sparingly' tip.

Nuts, Seeds, Beans, and Tofu: These are excellent sources of protein, fibre, vitamins, and minerals. Many kinds of nuts contain healthy fats, and some varieties (almonds, walnuts, peanuts, hazelnuts, and pistachios) are good for your heart.

Fish, Poultry, and Eggs: These are also important sources of protein. Since fish is rich in heart-healthy omega-3 fats eating fish can reduce the risk of heart disease.

Dairy Food: If you enjoy dairy foods, do so, but stick to one to two servings a day.

Use Sparingly: Red Meat, Processed Meat, and Butter: These foods contain lots of saturated fat, processed meat has been linked to increased risk of heart disease, diabetes, and colon cancer.

Use Sparingly: Refined Grains, Potatoes, Sugary Drinks, Sweets, Salt: These can cause increase in blood sugar that can lead to weight gain, diabetes, heart disease, and other chronic disorders.

There's just one basic guideline:

A healthy diet includes more foods from the base of the pyramid than from the higher levels of the pyramid.

Appendix 4

Bibliography

1. Agarwal, Dr. Yatish and Singh, Dr A P *Reversing Back Pain: Doctors' Guide to a Healthy Back* (New Delhi: Orient Paperbacks, 2008).
2. Agarwal, Dr. Yatish *The Body Talk* (New Delhi: Rupa & Co., 2000).
3. Hannaway, Dr. Paul J, *Asthma Self Help Book* (New Delhi: Orient Paperbacks, 1995).
4. Bakhru, H K *Foods That Heal* (New Delhi: Orient Paperbacks, 1990).
5. Bakhru, H K *Herbs That Heal* (New Delhi: Orient Paperbacks, 1990).
6. Bakhru, H K *Vitamins That Heal* (New Delhi: Orient Paperbacks, 1998).
7. Bauer, Joy *Food Cures* (USA: Rodale Books, 2007).
8. Bergner, Paul *Healing Power of Garlic* (New Delhi: Orient Paperbacks, 1998).
9. Bushman, Dr. Barbara A Editor, American College of Sports Medicine's *Complete Guide to Health and Fitness* (Human Kinetics, USA, 2011).
10. Carlson, K J, Eisenstat, Stephanie and Zipory, T *The New Harvard Guide to Women's Health* (Harvard University Press Reference Library, 1996).
11. Chambers, James; Chearney, Lee Ann; Romaine, S and Jewell, Cathy S *Facts on File* (New York: Health and Medicine, 2006)
12. Dandiya, Dr. P C; Bapna Dr. J S and Khilnani, Dr. G *The Complete Family Medicine Book,* 10th edition (New Delhi: Orient Paperbacks, 2011).
13. Gaderman, Peter Axt and Michaela Axt *The Joy of Laziness* (New Delhi: Orient Paperbacks, 2005).
14. Galbraith, Dr. Paul *Reversing Ageing* (New Delhi: Orient Paperbacks, 2006).
15. Gupta, Prof. Dr. Kishan *High Blood Cholesterol: Causes, Prevention & Treatment* (New Delhi: Orient Paperbacks, 1996).
16. Gupta, Prof. Dr. Kishan *High Blood Pressure: Causes, Prevention & Treatment* (New Delhi: Orient Paperbacks, 2007).
17. Jaggi, Dr. O P *Asthma & Allergies: Causes, Prevention & Treatment* (New Delhi: Orient Paperbacks, 1988).
18. Knopf, Dr. Karl *Weights for 50 +* (New Delhi: Orient Paperbacks, 2011).
19. Lin, Henry B *Chinese Health Care Secrets: A Natural Lifestyle Approach* (USA: Llewellyn Publications, 2000).

20. *Mayo Clinic Book of Home Remedies* (USA: Mayo Clinic 2010).
21. *Mayo Clinic Guide to Self Care* (New Delhi: Orient Paperbacks, 2004).
22. *Mayo Clinic on Healthy Ageing* (New Delhi: Orient Paperbacks, 2010).
23. Norfolk, Donald *Conquering Back Pain* (New Delhi: Orient Paperbacks, 1993).
24. Peale, Norman Vincent *Discovering the Power of Positive Thinking* (New Delhi: Orient Paperbacks, 2006).
25. Pollan, Michael *Food Rules: An Eater's Manual* (USA: Penguin Books, 2010).
26. Schriner, Dr Christian *Overcoming Stress* (New Delhi: Orient Paperbacks, 2000).
27. *Shahnaz Husain's Beauty Book* (New Delhi: Orient Paperbacks, 1991).
28. *ABCs of the Human Body: A Family Answer Book* (New York: Reader's Digest, 1986).
29. *The Lancet,* March, 2012.
30. Thomson, Robert *The Grosset Encyclopedia of Natural Medicine* (USA: Grosset and Dunlap, 1980).
31. Vodak, Paul *Preventing Heart Disease: Exercising for a Healthy Heart* (New Delhi: Orient Paperbacks, 1995).
32. Willett, Dr. Walter C and Skerrett, Patrick J *Eat, Drink and Be Healthy* (USA: Free Press/Simon and Schuster Inc., 2005).
33. Youngson, Dr R *Antioxidants: Vitamins C & E for Health* (New Delhi: Orient Paperbacks, 2000).

❐❐❐